The
Second
Circle

Also by Patsy Rodenburg

The Right to Speak: Working with the Voice
The Need for Words: Voice and the Text
The Actor Speaks: Voice and the Performer
Speaking Shakespeare

The Second Circle

How to Use Positive Energy for Success in Every Situation

This book will
transform your life,
minute to minute

Patsy Rodenburg

W. W. Norton & Company

New York · London

For information about permission to reproduce selections from this
book, write to Permissions, W. W. Norton & Company, Inc.,
500 Fifth Avenue, New York, NY 10110

For information about special discounts for bulk purchases, please
contact W. W. Norton Special Sales at specialsales@wwnorton.com
or 800-233-4830.

Manufacturing by R. R. Donnelley, Bloomsburg
Book design by Charlotte Staub
Production manager: Julia Druskin

Library of Congress Cataloging-in-Publication Data

Rodenburg, Patsy, 1953–
The second circle : how to use positive energy for success in every
situation : this book will transform your life, minute to minute /
Patsy Rodenburg.—1st American ed.
p. cm.
Previous title: "Presence : how to use positive energy for
success in every situation."
ISBN 978-0-393-06273-1 (hardcover)
1. Success. 2. Energy psychology. 3. Positive psychology. I. Title.

BF637.S8R583 2008
650.1—dc22

2007043533

W. W. Norton & Company, Inc.
500 Fifth Avenue, New York, N.Y. 10110
www.wwnorton.com

W. W. Norton & Company Ltd.
Castle House, 75/76 Wells Street, London W1T 3QT

1 2 3 4 5 6 7 8 9 0

To Michael

What is love? 'tis not hereafter;
Present mirth hath present laughter.

—WILLIAM SHAKESPEARE, *Twelfth Night*

Contents

Part Two: Living with Full Presence

Acknowledgments

Many people have supported me in writing this book, both professionally and personally.

Many thanks to Kate Adams for her faith in the book and to Bob Weil for his clear direction; to Joe Spieler and Arabella Stein for their constant energy; to my dear manager and friend Rick Scott, particularly for his patience; to Tyne Rafaeli for her diligence and fierce intelligence.

To a wonderful ensemble of friends and colleagues who have carried me on parts of the journey: Wendy Allnutt, Sue Barnet, Mary Carter, Martin Connor, Ian Cutts, Gil Dove, Anna Garduno, John Harle, Jenny Harris, Barry Ife, Wyn Jones, Brigid Larmour, Katie LeOrisa, Simon Mainwaring, Kelly McEvenue, Larry Moss, Lesley Murdin, Ruth Padel, Lisa Robertson, Max Rodenburg, Alaknanda Samarth, Mischa Scorer, Christina Shewell, Eliot Shrimpton.

To the great educators; my students at the Guildhall School of Music and Drama.

And lastly, to my dear Antonia Franceschi.

Introduction

This book will transform your life. This book will invigorate every aspect of your life. It will awaken your full human potential. It will change how you engage with others, how you look, listen, think, feel, learn, and do business. It will make you safer, challenge your compassion, your boredom, your negativity. You come into the world with hope and aliveness—born with positive presence. You will learn to remember and channel this vital energy into every aspect of your life.

To live life to its full Second Circle potential, you really need to allow yourself to return to the positive presence you were born with. This presence will make you more successful, more joyful and loving. It will change how you engage with others; how you look, listen, think, feel, and learn.

Here's the problem with the word "presence." Many people believe it is something you have or don't have. It's God-given, so that the charisma you see shimmering around a famous actor is not tangible and cannot be accessed. I don't agree: you might not have the makeup, clothes, and lighting effects that enhance the stars, but you can learn to find your own full charisma. All it is is energy. Present energy—clear, whole, and attentive energy.

This book and my quest for positive energy started thirty years ago. During those years, I have had the privilege to work with some of the most successful and famous performers on the planet. Perhaps more intriguingly, I have also worked not only with corporate leaders and those who serve society as teachers, doctors, and lawyers but with those who have fallen foul of it: prisoners. Let me explain.

Even when I was young, I loved the works of William Shakespeare and I feel blessed that I've been able to spend many years working with him. The more I worked with him the more I realized that I really loved his writing, not only because of the brilliance of his language or his profound understanding of human beings, but because he liked us. He really cared about people, knowing that we are more connected through our sameness than divided by our differences. More important, he asked us to behave better than we sometimes want to behave. Crucially, he revealed to us that we can only love unconditionally, find intimacy, be equal with each other, use power well, if we are present to each other and the world. Through trauma and loss he guides his characters onto a plane of positive presence.

I have traveled and worked all over the world. If people I meet on my travels hear that I work with Shakespeare, they will often quote one of his most famous lines: "To be or not to be: that is the question."

In this book I'm going to explore "To be or not to be" and prove that you have a choice, that you can live and be present positively in Second Circle with yourself and others. If you wish.

In 1977, I began teaching actors in a variety of colleges and theatre companies. In those early days I worked with some stars, but mainly with inexperienced young students. My job was to teach them voice, speech, and language skills. I found that getting them technically prepared was relatively straightforward, as they only had to learn and repeat certain exercises. But helping them to understand what they were saying and why they were saying it was harder, though with diligence it was obtainable.

They became audible, coherent, and interesting to listen to; yet that wasn't enough. I would sit and listen to maybe two hundred actors a week. I couldn't understand why certain actors did everything right yet didn't engage me or make me clear. Some were very impressive; they were clever and displayed intricate skills; but after watching them, I forgot their work—it didn't last in my memory. Some were very beautiful, but not connected enough to be sexually attractive. What was missing?

I questioned my elders, the more experienced teachers, about this, and they would smile and say something like, "It's talent, or 'presence.' So-and-so just hasn't got it." A tough notion, this "it." My colleagues seemed to be suggesting that if one hadn't already got it, getting it was beyond their power or mine to teach. The ones without it would presumably drop through some crack in the street and disappear forever. The flotsam and jetsam of life—the never-have-beens.

Now, what you should know about me at the beginning of this book is that I'm stubborn and have a heightened sense of fairness. I found the other teachers' reactions acutely unfair and I wasn't going to accept the inequality of human presence. What's more, once in a while, a student in one of my classes who initially didn't seem to have "it" would suddenly get "it." And if I acknowledged this transformation, some would keep it. Other teachers would notice and this failing student would start succeeding. Was this a miracle? I thought not. Even then I knew it wasn't a gift I was giving but an energy we all have; I had somehow enabled a student to find their true energy and this true energy was their presence. I set about searching how to define this presence and then how to enable my students to work with it.

Knowing that this process had something to do with energy, I began to recognize the different types of energy that a human being can learn to harness: energy of the body, the breath, the voice, the mind, the heart, and the spirit. We all give out energy and by listening we all receive energy. Give and take. What I discovered was that it wasn't a miracle that students found their presence, it was a tragedy that they had lost it in the first place. I began to know that presence is a universal quality that we all have but is somehow flattened out of us—"it" is a quality we all have locked away in our bodies and breath, which can be awakened.

Through formal exercises, I began to grasp that the energy of presence could be developed, understood, and enhanced. My instincts and my own fears told me that the energy of presence could only be cultivated and thrive in a safe arena. Even in the early days of the work I knew that presence in an individual is a life force that will dwindle when the force of negativity outweighs the positive in a working atmosphere. I actively discouraged behavior that, in my observations, diminished energy: carelessness, slouching, shallow breathing, underpowered voice, uninformed thinking, mocking and cynicism—anything that seemed to drain the vital life force out of a human being and the group around that person. Presence thrives amid unconditional love and joy.

Gradually, I identified three basic movements of energy. What I came to call the First Circle was inward-moving, drawing energy toward the self. At the opposite extreme was the Third Circle, in which energy is forced outward toward the world in general. In the Second Circle, energy was focused on a specific object or person and moved in both directions: taking in and giving out. Operating from within the Second Circle was what all the actors who possessed "it" had in common. Early on, I knew that the First Circle inward energy and the Third Circle generalized energy were useful to all of us, but the permanent loss of Second Circle in some of my students was the loss of their life force. I also knew that some people could manage Second Circle physically but not emotionally or intellectually: the real quest was to enable a fully functioning Second Circle human being.

I began to take this work out of the theatre and apply it to non-actors.

This part of the journey started when I was twenty-three. I had a telephone call from a lady, asking me to work with her brother. She sounded concerned but said only that he had a dull and boring voice.

"Yes," I said.

"He's old." She sounded embarrassed, and then she said, "He's not quite . . . normal."

"I'll try," I said.

"You're young . . . will you mind?"

"I'll try."

Her brother was called George; he was in his mid-fifties, neatly dressed—by his sister—shirt ironed, cardigan, woolen tie, polished shoes. He would sit upright, legs clamped together, hands clutching the armrest, knuckles white, forcing a smile to hide his fear and shame.

His voice was dead, but so were his eyes. He wasn't there—was it sedation? As my grandmother would have said, "There was no one home, no lights in the house." He tried to please me and perform his exercises and stretch the range of his voice—it didn't work.

I felt a failure, but his sister was delighted. Apparently, he loved coming to class. He got ready hours before the session . . . but he wasn't improving. I wanted to stop, only I needed the money!

Then, as spring came, I saw him two hours before the class, sitting in the square outside my apartment in rapture, gazing at a magnolia tree in bloom, and suddenly I *saw* George—he was there, present and alive. He was in Second Circle with the blossom.

After he shuffled into the apartment and we started the lesson, I asked, "What does the blossom make you feel?"

"Cathedrals," came the answer with a voice that soared like the Gothic vaulting he loved. He told me about the cathedrals he visited. He was fully present and fully engaged, his eyes focused.

"All that beauty falling down on you."

He finished and promptly absented himself from me and the world; but his cathedral passion had stage presence.

George taught me that it can be unlocked if I could find the key. A magnolia tree unlocked his presence. I did not have the opportunity or skills to transfer it to other parts of his life and I feared he lived mostly in First Circle—alone from the world—but for a moment, in front of me, George had presence, and then I knew without any doubt what Shakespeare knew: Every human being has presence and it is this universal human energy that unites us all.

It is learned habits that destroy our natural presence and connection to others and the world. Your presence is your natural state. Your habits are personal. George made me look again at the world and search for the Three Circles everywhere.

It was easier than I thought. They are around and within us in all social interactions. In every encounter, I noticed a person would come from one of the Three Circles of energy. No matter what their walk of life, those who were coming from Second Circle had a quality akin to stage presence. Like George and his magnolia blossom, they connected and felt "all there." Contact with such a person left me feeling enlivened.

In the thirty years since I first stumbled across these energies, I have taught them whenever and wherever I could. Whether the challenge was to win a patient's trust, manage a classroom full of unruly teenagers, close a sale, command the floor of the House of Commons, deal with hostile reporters, or survive in a maximum-security prison, the clear winners were those with presence. In fact, you can't win anything without it; even if it only visits you for a moment, it is the moment that will change your life. Those who are branded "losers" have only lost their presence.

Anyone can acquire the elusive quality that actors call "it." The theory is easily grasped—almost deceptively simple—but its application requires lots of practice, particularly if you want it to stay permanently. Exercises and exercising will enable you to hone every aspect of presence: posture, breath, voice, sensory awareness, listening, clear thinking, generosity of heart, and sheer bravery. This book explains how "staying in Second" can be applied to both mundane and extraordinary life challenges.

Whenever I teach, I always say to my students that I realized many years ago I have discovered nothing new in the world. Everything I teach and write about is already known. You really do "know" about presence, and somewhere, perhaps buried deep within you, is a memory of that. I truly know this book will ignite you into your full presence.

You don't need to rush. Take your time. Some of the exercises are difficult, but you needn't punish yourself for finding them so. Some of the exercises you might not fully understand, but don't worry. No one can rush deep learning. You will notice that I have used quotes to highlight certain areas of the work. Some of them will be coming off the wall at you. Enjoy them even if you don't immediately understand their relevance, because you might do so eventually.

All you need do if you want to transform your life is work—and you and I *will* work. But before we do so, I think we should dwell on presence and Second Circle and how well you already understand this energy. Why do you need it? We should remind ourselves why we lost our presence. You know it wasn't your fault that it left you. Someone or something took it from you. Now you are going to take it back.

Part One

Finding
Your
Presence

1

Presence

Only connect!

—E. M. FORSTER, *Howards End*

Take time to remember, however distant those memories are, your experiences of Second Circle: the moments when your energy fully connected you to the world and you received energy back from that connection. It could be a second, catching the eye of a stranger, or the longer, unabashed gaze you can share with a baby. Remember your equivalent of George's magnolia or the shock and awe of meeting a tiger's eyes at the zoo.

Remember that jolt of energy, akin to electricity, that flicks a switch in your whole body if you are driving without full attention and a child runs out into the street, and you can only hit the brakes if you find your presence. Or think of the energy you feel if you are followed by a stalker and you need presence to outwit him (or her). Or the surge of energy when you catch a stranger's eye and share a moment. Or that moment when you understand an idea, the clouds part in the mind, and light enters—you can only be enlightened when you are present. Equally, you can only experience an emotion totally if you are present to a feeling—and you remember forever the textures of present feelings—as you experience the bad news, the good news, or shocking news.

As you read this book, pull yourself into your presence, what I call the Second Circle, and start a lifelong journey with me to reconnect. Presence allows experience, and all the messages and tools required to survive physically, intellectually, and emotionally are taught when you are present.

It is the energy of survival. When you are not present you can be in danger, whether you are in the jungle or closer to home at work and with your family.

Second Circle is also intimacy. Two human beings present together experience intimacy and knowledge of one another; each person understands something of the other's story and, consequently, their humanity. This humanity can be experienced in a touch, the breath, the voice—but it is immediately felt and seen through the eyes: the windows of the soul.

This explains why executioners avoid looking into the eyes of their victims. Historically, hoods are placed over prisoners' heads or they are shot from behind. Legend has it that one of the reasons Heinrich Himmler ordered the development of gas chambers for the Third Reich ethnic cleansing campaign was to avoid German soldiers' inevitable connection with their victims. Himmler knew that too many connections between soldier and victim could derail the Final Solution.

Armies are painstakingly drilled, partly to obey orders but partly to be sufficiently dehumanized to who or why they are killing. If that doesn't work, alcohol or drugs will do the trick— hard to be present when you are "out of your mind."

A family story goes that at the terrible Battle of the Somme in World War I, my grandfather shared a cigarette with an enemy German soldier in no-man's-land. Sitting in the mud in a shell crater, they spent an hour in silent communion. Before this hour of harmony they had met each other, bayonets fixed, arms trained to lunge and kill; but through their fear and their different uniforms, helmets, and filthy faces, they caught each other's eyes and just chose to sit and smoke a cigarette. I have to add it was a decision that could have had my grandfather Jimmy shot at dawn for cowardice—the end of him and me!

Fighters skilled in killing with machines and technology can now kill without risk of being present to and with their enemies. But even in modern wars, you hear similar stories. As soldiers get closer to their enemy, they are more vulnerable to being present with them and having "doubts." Those who have been close to any killing are more likely to be anti-war than those cheering, unpresent to it, on the sidelines.

> If in smothering dreams you too could pace
> Behind the wagon that we flung him in,
> And watch the white eyes writhing in his face,
> His hanging face, like a devil's sick of sin;
> If you could hear, at every jolt, the blood
> Come gargling from the froth-corrupted lungs,
> Obscene as cancer, bitter as the cud
> Of vile, incurable sores on innocent tongues,—
> My friend, you would not tell with such high zest
> To children ardent for some desperate glory,
> The old Lie: Dulce et decorum est
> Pro patria mori.*
>
> —WILFRED OWEN, "Dulce et Decorum Est"

So many movies explore the moment when the really hard hit man makes eye contact with his victim and cannot kill her.

Falling in love or lust occurs across crowded rooms when two people are fully present with each other. This is what happens to Romeo and Juliet: a presence with each other so strong that it is more real to them than family, duty, and the fear of death. In the present, you meet someone's eyes and are changed; they know and you know. Two people really meeting, not glancing off each other, but an intoxicating and rich event that travels with us even if you never meet again or even know the person's name. A few moments that remain with you for years.

In 1987, while walking on a beach in southern India, I met a stranger walking in the opposite direction. We made eye contact and stopped and chatted to each other. We walked together, sat

---

* Latin for "It is sweet and meet to die for one's country."

and looked across the Indian Ocean. A meeting of two cultures; a present meeting.

Like my grandfather's meeting with an enemy soldier, we were together just an hour, and then we parted. No names were exchanged. I have a photograph—too precious to show anyone. Years have passed, but I still yearn to be on that beach again with that stranger. This can only be described as love, and I'm willing to wager that many of you have had a similar experience but cannot speak of it; after all, who would understand? You were fully present, and that memory heightens the lack of daily presence you feel. There is no more present a sound than a baby's first cry. This compulsive cry states, "I'm here, help me!"

In the beginning and once upon a time you were present, and correctly so. King Lear has to go on a humbling journey from absolute power to naked beggar. At that point he knows and feels his own presence and its connection to being a baby:

. . . we came crying hither.
Thou know'st the first time that we smell the air
We wawl and cry.

Babies and toddlers are present almost constantly. Watch a baby or toddler discover the world around them and you are watching positive energy; then witness the thrilling experience of their eyes looking into yours. In that moment even the most jaded adult is brought back to life.

Child-rearing books advise the parents to communicate with their toddler face to face. This places the adult in a position where being present with their child is more possible. Because presence is a child's natural state, children will tend to listen more clearly and respond.

A mother's present connection to her baby is so powerful that partners can feel neglected and lonely. After the connection diminishes, some mothers long for another baby to reexperience that connection. A recent study of adolescent pregnancy suggested that young girls repeatedly become pregnant because they feel alive and needed by their baby. As the child moves away from them, they have another baby to reconnect to that feeling of aliveness–presence.

Even the most physically impaired people can rediscover their powerful Second Circle.

My dear sister Susan, after she had suffered a mentally damaging stroke, displayed her true loving instincts.

Susan, her small daughter, my mother, and I were walking in the local park.

After the trauma of her stroke, Susan was in a daze. Lost in a deep First Circle, she wandered along the leafy paths, her small daughter trotting excitedly in front of us. We arrived at a duck pond.

These things happen so quickly. Suddenly little Katie was in the water. Now, I can move fast, if required, but just as my first leg was knee-deep in the pond, I was overtaken by a streak of dynamic energy. *Splash.* Susan had gathered her child out of the water and was holding her close. The amazing maternal instinct threw Susan out of her First Circle oblivion into a heightened Second Circle. Her love propelled her into a place that clinical expectations had deemed impossible.

Literature yields similar moments. In George Eliot's *Silas Marner*, a lonely, isolated, and despairing miser is brought back to life when an orphaned infant toddles into his cottage:

In old days there were angels who came and took men by the hand and led them away from the city of destruction. We see no white-winged angels now. But yet men are led away from threatening destruction: a hand is put into theirs, which leads them forth gently towards calm and bright land, so that they look no more backward; and the hand may be a little child's.

Animals, like babies and toddlers, often have the same effect. Indeed, you regularly receive presence from animals. Dogs are constantly present. Cats are, too, but pretend they are not really interested in your presence. Studies now prove that people living alone with an animal are happier than those who have no pets and no one to care for, or to care for them. The presence of a pet pulls you into Second Circle. The pet tells you that you are needed. It is a shared acceptance that your life is happening and that it matters. The horse whisperer has learned to be fully present to the horse and the horse feels this energy. The horse is not "broken" but obeys through mutual respect and equality. Across many cities in Britain you see the homeless with their dogs, both lost but both found in each other; companions of despair but at least present with each other.

Great performers work in this state. If you remember a performance days after experiencing it, it means the performer was present and you were present receiving the work.

Sometimes, you understand presence by its very absence. An unpresent star on stage means that the audience's eye refocuses on an actor *with* presence—who may be outshining a Hollywood star who isn't using "it." The theatre world is full of terrible stories about stars having smaller-part actors fired because the unknown actor has presence, shares a scene with the star, and draws all the attention of the audience away from them. They equal the stories of the present actors working extra hard to hide a star's lack of stage charisma.

It is always dangerous to act with a child or an animal on stage. They are constantly present, and unless you are too, even a dog will outshine you.

When I was five, my mother took me to the theatre to see Shakespeare's comedy *The Two Gentlemen of Verona*. There is a dog called Crab in the play. The dog shares two scenes with a character called Launce. I can't say I remember the actor's performance but it must have been one of those overacted caricatured comedy performances totally unrelated to any human truth. After the show I asked my mother, "Why was the dog real and the man not?"

Great athletes win with presence. Every great sporting success is one of being present and every failure involves some momentary lack of presence. No one wins a gold medal without fantastic talent and physical skill, but a champion also has a supreme ability to stay focused in the present. Watch athletes line up for a race and note the ones not pulled away from their presence by a movement in the crowd or a false start. Watch a superior tennis player lose a vital game because they were distracted by a bad line call. Watch a team fail because one member fails to be properly present.

Every great communicator speaks from this place. For good or ill, great orators can change the world. The powerful leaders of countries or companies have presence. Martin Luther King, Jr., and Adolf Hitler can be taken as examples of opposite ends of the scale. During a crisis, presence in the leader is essential. Those who are being led will only feel safe and confident if they feel connected to their leader. The British needed Winston Churchill in World War II and the United States needed John F. Kennedy during the Cuban missile crisis. Both had powerful presence and both led their countries through crisis.

Great healers can only wholly heal if they are present with their patients. Humanitarian work is often pursued by those who have seen the pain of others and truly empathized with it.

An example of this is a nineteenth-century reformer by the name of Elizabeth Fry. This courageous woman, criticized by other women of her time for having such an influential social role and neglecting her duties as a wife, helped to reform Britain's prisons. In 1812, she visited Newgate Prison and really saw the horrific conditions people were kept in, even before their trials. This moment changed Fry, and eventually the penal system. This privileged woman must have been in Second Circle to see the suffering of those whom most women in her class would have perceived as lower beings.

If you want others to be happy, practice compassion. If you want to be happy, practice compassion.   —THE DALAI LAMA

Spiritual teachers are present; if they are not, we instinctively distrust their spirituality and their teachings. But even within our own daily lives no relationship can work without partners, family, and work colleagues who are present with each other.

Remember the teachers who changed your life? They were present, and through that energy made you connect with learning. Even if you started out with no particular interest in their subject, they drew you in with their passion and energy. Conversely, you might have had the experience of loving a subject, but because the teacher was so boring, or lacking in presence, your passion was dulled, if not lost forever.

Being present is thrilling, inspiring, absorbing, surprising, and even frightening, all at the same time. It is the energy you feel when you know you are alive, the energy of those moments that writers write about, singers sing about, and the dying remember on their deathbeds. We all yearn to be present and to be met by others who are equally present. We are lonely without these encounters. Presence enables you to honor, understand, and empathize with others. A leader's presence inspires confidence in followers. A parent's presence makes children feel cherished and secure. A lover's presence thrills and satisfies the beloved. When fully present in your spiritual life, you encounter the divine.

Think about this: You know when others are not present with you. You feel ignored, dismissed, unimportant, and detached from your surroundings. You feel alone in a relationship when your partner is not present with you. Lovemaking becomes just sex. A candlelit dinner for two becomes lonely and disturbing when one or both of you are not present. Walking into a party at which no one recognizes your presence becomes a humiliating experience. The streets of your neighborhood are dangerous when you walk them without being present to others. The meeting at work becomes infuriating when you speak and no one hears you. A doctor talking about your body and well-being without connecting with you is alarming. A priest not present at a loved one's funeral, speaking in patronizing generalities, makes the grief worse. No relationship can work—be it with partners, children, friends, or colleagues—without both parties being fully present with each other. So, if you know when others are not present with you, then they too will know when you are not there!

When I first read the Bible, it puzzled me that God asked Adam in the Garden of Eden, "Where are you, Adam?" As a six-year-old I couldn't understand why the all-seeing God didn't see Adam hiding behind a tree. Much later I realized that God was asking Adam a question about presence, where he was in himself. God asked Adam to be present, awake, alive, and conscious of his actions: "Where are you?" Adam wasn't there.

Presence is the energy that comes from you and connects you to the outside world. It is essential to your survival when you are threatened. It is the heart of intimacy between people, and although you can live in your inner world without presence in yourself, the outer world we live in will appear dull, stale, and flat. It is when you are fully present that you do your best work and make your deepest impression.

You will also realize that being present to life is critical not only to your well-being but to the well-being of everyone around you. It is an act of community. It is an act of personal intimacy with others. It enables not only the success of an individual but also the success of a family, society, and team. It is what being in Second Circle is all about.

We make a living by what we get, we make a life by what we give.   —Sir Winston Churchill

2

How Is Presence Lost?

Some people, often out of a need to control, don't want your presence, so it has been knocked out of you. At other times life is too easy, so why bother to be present? And sometimes life is so hard that you need to unplug the present life force just to stop the pain.

None of the above is your fault, but you do have the power to reinstate presence into your life, particularly if you feel that your life is drained of meaning, intensity, and joy. What stops your presence can seem out of your immediate control.

Urban living crams hundreds of strangers into your life. To be present with all these strangers is impossible and even dangerous. Anthropologists suggest our species is not programmed to meet thousands of people. We are programmed to encounter and know a few hundred in a life, and then not on a daily basis. No wonder, as you hurry though crowds on the street, or are crammed in a train carriage, or work in an organization where few know your name, or are educated in a school and college where you suspect no one notices if you go missing, that you close down your presence. So, the temptation as you rush through crowds is to close down even more. You will always be more present in rural surroundings, on a country walk, greeting the few passing strangers you meet, noticing them and the world around. Here you can reconnect to nature and your present nature.

Paradoxically, many of the comforts and conveniences of modern life are obstacles to being present. Any threats to your survival command your complete and immediate attention. When confronted with danger, there is no possibility of *not* being present. The loss of contact with nature in many lives and the ease that technology offers have made us lazy to immediate survival needs and have numbed our senses. The devices that are meant to help connect us with the world—computers, televisions, cars, and cell phones—serve to isolate us, rendering our contacts more numerous and then more superficial.

An image I have of our twenty-first-century lifestyle is that we have fully relaxed into a large, cushioned couch, and this comfort makes it more difficult to get up and confront the arrival of a malevolent intruder in the home. The cushioned comfort has put our survival presence to sleep. Many of us are like fat cats, safe by the fire, paws and claws tucked away under our chins.

Some years ago, I was working with Hopi Native Americans. One of the elders said something so simple and direct that I remember it to this day. He noted that the Hopi, being nomadic, seek hardship; if life gets too easy in a certain environment, they move on to a harder place and life.

"Why?" I asked.

"If life is too easy, you lose your joy."

No one in our society wishes to have a harder life. Therefore, to experience presence and joy it is necessary to spend time each day staying present, and struggling free from the cushioned comforts of our lifestyles, which can so easily smother presence.

The loss of presence in general society means that our economy thrives. Materialism, to some extent, requires that the consumer is not fully present or happy. In the moments of a spending frenzy you feel more alive so you spend, spend, spend in the pursuit of happiness. For a short period the acquisition of clothes, shoes, a house, a car, a new kitchen, anchors your life into some place of meaning.

You can also lose your quality of presence through physical, emotional, intellectual, or spiritual pain. In pain, our natural and necessary inclination is to dull the experience by withholding full attention and engagement from the world or bluffing through the pain by pushing the world away from us. If we don't return to the world when the pain thaws, we may stay disconnected for the rest of our lives. In this way, an ancient pain can distance you throughout the remainder of your life.

We all know that one of the most successful ways to stop pain and presence is to drink or use other drugs. The reason that drunks are dangerous and boring is that they are not there with you, but are lost in another world. Driving when drunk is destructive because you are not present to the road and the traffic around you. You are not in a place of survival and your inability to survive could harm others.

Marriages fail when partners no longer feel the intimacy of being present with each other. Affairs are started to try to recapture the excitement of intimacy. Children lose contact with their parents, and vice versa, when there is no present living moment in the family.

You change careers, go traveling, play extreme sports, get plastic surgery, drive fast cars, take exotic holidays, or redecorate the house, constantly seeking presence. These strategies might work for an hour, a day, or a year, but they will not solve your inner deadness. To do that, you have to work to understand your energy and to be present in Second Circle.

3

The Three Circles of Energy

To go beyond is as wrong as to fall short.

—CONFUCIUS

A natural movement of energy should always run through you. Body, breath, voice; how you listen, think, and feel. You feel this energy and others feel it around you. This energy is completely tangible. Read the list below carefully:

- The Three Circles of Energy describe the three basic ways human energy moves.
- The movement of energy is all through your body, breath, voice, and how you listen, think, and feel.
- You feel this energy as do others around you. In this way, the energy is completely tangible.
- You can move through all Three Circles rapidly within seconds. The speed and shifts in energy can be startling.
- You need to be able to access all Three Circles during the course of the day.
- The Three Circles describe energy, not the content of that energy. So you can experience any thought or emotion in any of these Circles with different degrees of intensity.
- You have a favorite Circle, one that is habitual to you, and it is this favorite energy that is blocking your presence.

Please remember that the state of presence is your birthright, so when you discover the energy you live in most, don't despair. This right will overcome the habit.

I am deliberately outlining First and Third Circle before Second Circle. First and Third take you out of your natural presence of Second Circle. As we are all aiming for Second Circle presence, this is the final Circle we will be looking at in this chapter.

First Circle: The Circle of Self and Withdrawal

Here, your whole focus is inward. The energy you generate falls back into you. First Circle absorbs other people's energy and draws all outward stimulus inward. When in First Circle, you are not very observant or perceptive about people or objects outside yourself. They interest you only as a means to clarify yourself, not the world around you.

At its best, First Circle is the energy of introspection and reflection. This is very useful at times, but to live predominantly in First Circle is very limiting, if not disabling. You can come across to others as self-centered, uncaring, and withdrawn, and you tend to drain rather than enliven others. Your personal power and impact on the world is compromised and you are vulnerable to being victimized.

You are in First Circle if you

- Find yourself withdrawing physically from people, feelings, or ideas
- Find you are holding your breath or breathing rapidly and shallowly
- Are asked to repeat yourself when you speak
- Find that people lean forward to hear you or notice you
- Are frequently ignored, and not missed when you leave a room
- Feel left out

- Often feel self-conscious
- Wear clothes that help you not to be noticed

By drawing energy inward, you lessen your impact on the world, but you also put yourself in danger as you are not fully noticing your surroundings.

First Circle is useful when you don't want to be noticed. You can watch the most flamboyant actors adopt this energy as they try to slip out of the stage door without being stopped for an autograph. A famous story about Marilyn Monroe tells how she was shopping in a busy store with her friend. The friend was amazed that no one recognized her. Marilyn then showed her friend how she could suddenly *be* Marilyn: she switched herself on—and was immediately swamped by fans. She went from First Circle into her presence and was immediately noticed.

If you live constantly in First Circle, your passion for life has been dulled. You are shy.

As you read this book you might realize that when you work with a hobby or get fully engaged with a passion, you will abandon First Circle and enter your presence. Great writers might be shy in public but they write their books with full presence.

You may be living in First Circle because you were chased back out of your presence by criticism, unwelcome attention, or abuse. You have learned to hide your visibility and not be noticed.

Third Circle: The Circle of Bluff and Force

In Third Circle, all of your energy is outward-moving and non-specific, and is untargeted. It is as if you are spraying your energy out to the world with an aerosol can. Your attention is outside yourself, yet unfocused, lacking precision and detail. You get a loose connection to any situation, but miss the nuances. The world is a dimly lit audience for whom you are performing.

In Third Circle you attract attention, and you may even make a favorable first impression. This is deceptively useful in situations where you need to engage superficially with people in groups and gain their immediate compliance or cooperation. It's good for getting parties started, and for rallying the troops. The drawback is that you are not engaging specifically with anything and therefore cannot take energy back in. This energy lacks intimacy; others feel that they don't really matter to you and therefore the energy is impersonal to them. In Third Circle, you may speak eloquently, sound enthusiastic and charming, but you don't listen well. You look through people rather than at them, skimming the surface of every interaction.

Third Circle is a forceful shield that protects you and your vulnerability from the intrusions of the world, and you will sometimes need to hold that shield up to the world. If, however, this energy is the norm, you are not receiving any energy from the world. You are alone and fighting to control your life without allowing anyone to help. At worst, others experience you as insensitive, arrogant, and overbearing.

You are in Third Circle if you

- Notice people withdrawing from you or making space for you
- Find yourself taking up more space than you need
- Breathe with noise, pulling the air into your body and taking the oxygen from others
- Are told often that you are too loud, either in speech or laughter
- Don't really notice the people you are speaking to or the room you are in
- Don't notice if people are not enjoying themselves as you are
- Feel that you have to inject energy into every social event at any price to yourself and others
- Take command of a discussion even if you have only heard

a fragment of what is being discussed, so that you are
accused of interrupting others
- Wear clothes that get you noticed

Third Circle has its uses. You can enter this circle to protect
yourself, channeling the energy out from yourself and keeping
others at bay. Passing through a crowd is a physical example of
this. If ever I'm in a pressing crowd that I need to pass through, I
listen for a loud voice going my way and follow in its wake. The
loud voice is an indication of Third Circle, and the individual
with that voice has no problems pushing his or her way through
others. Third Circle energy can stop an unwanted conversation
or intrusion and defend your privacy. You can be pleasant and
enthusiastic without fully committing to people.

People working in the service industries are normally highly
skilled in Third Circle. They have to feign charm and concern for
hundreds of others. It is actually impossible to do this and still
be fully present with all those strangers. So the solution is Third
Circle. Royalty and celebrities keep a distance from their public
with Third Circle energy, pushing strangers away. In these cases
they pretend intimacy but stay defended.

If you know you fall into a Third Circle habit, it is probably
because your back was pushed up against the wall at some time
in your life and you came out fighting! You were desperate to
be felt and seen, not reduced and ignored.

Maybe now you will realize you don't have to fight all the
time.

Second Circle: The Energy of Connecting

In Second Circle, your energy is focused. It moves out toward
the object of your attention, touches it, and then receives energy
back from it. You are living in a two-way street—you give to
and are responsive with that energy, reacting and communicat-

ing freely. You are in the moment—in the so-called "zone"—and
moment to moment you give and take. Both giving and taking, in that moment, are equal to each other. In Second Circle,
you touch and influence another person rather than impress
or impose your will on them. You influence them by allowing
them to influence you. You hear others and take in what they
are really saying. Second Circle energy, when positive, is generous. It begets intimacy.

When the power and precision of Second Circle energy is
fueled by malice or darker emotions, then the receiver is in real
danger. Second Circle is inappropriate when it touches people
who do not want to fully engage with you. Those who have no
clear path of escape from you (such as students or employees)
will experience it as invasive.

Positive presence through Second Circle is the most powerful,
creative, and intimate way of interacting with the world. The art
of being present is the art of operating from Second Circle.

You know you are in Second Circle if you

- Feel centered and alert
- Feel your body belongs to you
- Feel the earth through your feet
- Feel your breath is easy and complete
- Know you reach people and they hear you when you speak
- Notice details in others—their eyes, their moods, their
  anxieties
- Are curious about a new idea—not judgmental
- Hear clearly
- Acknowledge the feelings of others
- See, hear, smell, touch something new, which focuses this
  energy in the whole of you

In Second Circle you are noticed, heard, remembered—and
powerful. This focus of clear energy has its problems. Let's go

back and begin to appreciate how dangerous your present power might be to others around you.

A weak father doesn't really want his son to challenge him with presence. Children are told not to stare or show too much interest in certain things. Cultural factors come into play. Some women are punished for not being in First Circle. In some countries, the release of Second Circle emotion is encouraged; in others, it is thought to be distasteful. In some families, certain subjects are never discussed in Second Circle. When I first taught in India, I realized I was asking women teachers to be in Second Circle, which was completely against their upbringing. I was equally shocked to teach Second Circle to emotionally expressive Russians—very different from their less emotionally expressive English counterparts.

I am telling you all this to make you extremely aware of how clever you can be in hiding your Second Circle.

Remember the experience of standing at a party talking to someone you feel obliged to please and being bored by them but too polite to move away, even if you are more interested in someone across the room. You act and mask a charming Third Circle to the person you are with, but your Second Circle energy is attached to the person across the room. You don't need to look at them; you can feel and connect with them across space with your Second Circle energy. And what about those occasions when you overhear people gossiping? You long to hear what they are saying but know that they won't include you. You act as if you are concentrating on a task like tidying your desk, but your real focused Second energy is on their conversation.

I learned very quickly when I started to teach children with speech impediments to get them physically helping me with a task like stacking books or chopping a carrot—anything to dupe them into thinking my whole attention wasn't on them. In this way they were freed from feeling a Second Circle scrutiny on their speech problem and 80 percent of the time this freedom from scrutiny enabled them to speak without an impediment. We would chat away, and after a while I would say, "You know you haven't stuttered for twenty minutes." And they hadn't!

Historically, servants have had to learn to perform this mix of energy in order to serve but not intrude and this is a form of survival. It is a way of keeping your job with difficult and demanding employers. A good waiter serves you attentively at lunch, seemingly not hearing your conversation, but in fact alert to your every need. He is deliberating flattening himself into First Circle, but that actually masks a strong Second Circle attention on you.

My mother was brilliant at eavesdropping. On returning from family meals in restaurants, she would report in painstaking detail the conversations that were occurring on tables around ours. A sad reflection on her interest in her own family's mealtime conversations!

Recently, a friend and I were having a very intense and personally revealing discussion in the back of a taxi. Neither of us noticed the driver; he seemed completely preoccupied in driving. But when she left the cab, he turned to me and commented on what we had been talking about. I felt foolish and duped. By forgetting the driver's presence—however well disguised—I had handed a stranger intimate information about both our lives.

The fashion of "cool" is a studied physical manifestation of First Circle. If it was a true First Circle, then in the state of cool you are not aware of anyone around you. You are completely self-involved. Mostly, cool is a First Circle front hiding an acute Second Circle attention to the world. There is a historic suggestion that the term "cool" comes from the black American slave who didn't dare look at or challenge the master, let alone the mistress. The front of this "cool" is a display of physical powerlessness, to avoid punishment but actually stay highly tuned in Second Circle to survive a ruthless owner. Sitting on a London tube train or New York subway late at night it is very advisable to manifest First Circle but stay alert to the whole car in Second Circle. Teaching in prisons, I have seen this energy mix very clearly. Most inmates want to stay out of trouble, so they feign First Circle but actually must be in Second Circle.

Cool is only destructive if it has completely closed you down in First. You can observe this in privileged children, who manifest the cool shutdown because they have a highly acute understanding of energy levels, without ever knowing that they should stay attentive if they want to survive.

When I have taught groups of prostitutes, they understand this energy mix well. They have to please and flatter their clients, so pretend an intimate connection to them in Second Circle. In fact, they are really surviving by being in Second Circle with their surroundings and in First Circle with the client. They have no interest in intimacy with a paying customer. Paying for sex is a transaction that is devoid of equality. Who actually has the upper hand in this deal is up for debate. High-class prostitutes can believe they do; the more desperate and less protected know otherwise. As you work in Second Circle more, you will know when others are feigning an energy, but only if you are in Second Circle yourself.

What Are You? Where Are You?

I think by now you have a good idea of your favorite Circle and how often you are present in the world. Please remember that you are using every Circle but do have a habitual one. Take time and make a list of all the most important people in your life. Here is an example:

Parents   Partners   Teachers   Friends
Children   Siblings   Colleagues

Is there any specific pattern of energy to your interaction with each of these people? Who is present with you? Who allows your presence? Who blocks it?

Here are some questions to consider:

Do you experience Second Circle equal intimacy with anyone? Who? How often?

Does Second Circle frighten you? Does it thrill you?

Do you trust in Second Circle?

Can you love in Second Circle?

Are there tasks that take away your presence?

Are there sports or pastimes that focus you into Second
Circle?

I don't expect you to be able to answer all these questions right away, but I think even answering three or four will begin to bring together pieces of a jigsaw or glass in a stained-glass window. A pattern and shape to your energy will emerge, and with that will come an awareness of patterns of energy around you.

Over days, weeks, and even years, you will find answers to more of these questions, and with these answers you will begin to understand the impact you have on the world and its impact on you. You will begin to shift out of habits that tie you down, and to move energy in yourself and others with ease and fluidity.

4

How to Move into Second Circle

There are certain topics that have many people fidgeting and wriggling in their seats. This is a sure sign of unease, if not distress. Isn't it wonderful that ideas can produce such physical reactions? The discomfort comes from fear, and fear can create knee-jerk reactions in even the most reasonable individual.

So, what are these topics, and why am I proposing ideas that will cause distress? First, the topics:

Transformation: Well, a lot of people don't like change, but change is inevitable. Even if your stuck habits *feel* safe, they are not;

Power: Many of us are frightened of power, mistaking it for force, and even those with power are uneasy discussing it. All our deep fears about power are due to its potential misuse by us or against us;

Gender: Both men and women are tired of discussing the differences, but the basic issues have not yet been resolved, only repositioned.

Why do I feel compelled to discuss these subjects? Well, Second Circle presence is about being in the moment, and being in the moment keeps you open to change. Presence is constantly undergoing a process of transformation. Then, to be intimate with others in Second Circle requires both parties knowing that they are equal. No one can assume superiority in intimacy. Hence the discussions of power and gender.

Please don't feel uneasy—but try to bear with me here.

Transformation

Transformation is uncomfortable and in a totally practical way requires constant reminders in the body, mind, and heart. Even seemingly small, unimportant changes can take time. Recently, I had my kitchen floor lowered, which meant one of the steps up from the kitchen was higher. Training my body to realign itself to those two extra inches was startling. Coming down I was continually offbalance and going up often made me trip. It took conscious effort to negotiate a kitchen step.

A friend of mine who had been a gymnast, then trained as a high diver, had to work with intense concentration to remember to enter the water headfirst. Her body had been trained to land through every somersault on her feet. The concept of entering the water the other way around required complete concentration.

My ex-husband, a very visual man, noticed to his horror that when I looked at paintings in galleries, I read the title before looking at the work. It took me years to train myself out of that one. I have to confess that I now enjoy the paintings more by looking first rather than reading their titles.

These examples are really trivial, but you must acknowledge that most of your energy habits have been developed for your survival. Therefore, releasing a different and perhaps more real aspect of yourself will take courage and some discomfort.

You might know about the ring of fire—an image used in forms of alternative healing. Many of us are metaphorically standing in a ring of fire. The assaults of life have pushed us through a wall of fire and here we are, standing in the middle of a circle of flames. The conundrum we face in the circle is: would we rather spend the rest of our lives very uncomfortable, hot and singed, or do we have the courage to walk through the wall of flames again, experiencing a short burning sensation, to freedom from fire?

The benefits of being in Second Circle are infinite, but the transformation can feel like a journey through a wall of flames. A habitual Third Circle person can feel very exposed and vulnerable as he or she moves from Third to Second.

The Move from Third to Second

If you think you are a Third Circle person, then this transformation becomes particularly problematic if you believe that Third represents your power and defends you. You might, deep down, believe that you are superior to either your family, colleagues, or neighbors.

Maybe you feel that by being in Third you are protected from attack, emotional connection, ridicule, and failure, and to a certain extent Third does shield you from all of the above. However, you might have already realized that this defense also keeps you away from any meaningful engagement, and thus you probably feel lonely when in Third for any extended length of time.

When in Third Circle, you are pushing yourself into and onto the world before the world can meet, hurt, or love you. You feel in more control in Third but actually are using force to get your way, and you should know that when your back is turned there is likely to be an insurrection at work or in the home. You can intimidate people around you and you might misinterpret their reaction as respect. The Third Circle energy is hard to respect as it doesn't allow others to contribute anything to you, and it's hard to like. The people who stay around you for any length of time do so not because they are willing but because you control them. The Second Circle two-way street does not exist for you. It is possible that you have convinced yourself that you don't need people and that your loneliness is a choice.

As you move into Second Circle you will feel that you are relinquishing power, but actually what you are relinquishing is brute force, and your status will grow. Allowing equality with others will inevitably feel uncomfortable; but if Second lives in you even for a short while, you will discover qualities in people you have never observed or really known. This can only be good for your and others' well-being and survival.

In Second Circle you will begin to forge quality and caring relationships, even with people you have known superficially for years. You will begin to notice the truth of other people's responses to you. With this clarity you will have more success in your relationships at home and at work—you might even be promoted. All the extra vulnerability you offer will be rewarded with a greater satisfaction in life.

Now, you could be one of those Third Circle people who use this energy to shield a deeper sense of inferiority. You are a direct antithesis to the superior Third Circle energy. Your Third Circle is charged with false enthusiasm, relentless charm and jollity, and your sense of burning unease is charged with fear of being ignored or disliked.

You might be frightened that transforming into Second Circle could reveal that you are not liked. We all know that it is impossible to make people like us. People like us or don't; but it is more possible to like someone in Second because they are there for us.

Relentless Third Circle charm and enthusiasm are tiring for you and for others. As you begin to transform into Second Circle, you will find that many people are more willing to connect to you and shallow acquaintances will disperse. In Second you are less open to attack and, should you ever need it, a Third shield can be rapidly deployed.

The Move from First to Second

Transformation from First to Second energy has other problems. The fear is that you will be noticed and even asked
to participate. In First you might feel lonely, but you also
feel safe and don't have to engage, share, or take responsibility for your presence in the world. As you move into
Second Circle, your presence will be felt and you might have
to examine and face what made you withdraw from it. This
may be some sort of criticism or, even worse, abuse. You must
bear in mind that if you don't return to Second Circle, the negativity that made you retreat in the first place will be trium-
phant. Life will daze you, not invigorate you.

Even after a short time in Second, your self-consciousness
will begin to fade and others will find you more effective
and credible. Gradually, you will feel more actively useful and acknowledged in the world, and you will be noticed
positively.

Or, you might be one of those First Circle people who can't
really be bothered to join the world. Maybe the people around
you even feel inferior to you. Or maybe you have perfected an
aura of First Circle cool to hide your passion. The trouble with
this is you can't be trusted and eventually the First Circle energy
will kill your passions.

If you lead a group in First Circle, your energy will deaden
theirs, and everyone's productivity will fade. All great leaders
are in Second Circle with their passions, so you, in First, can
only produce mediocrity in yourself and others.

As you move into Second Circle you might feel ridiculous,
humiliated, and exposed, but if you do, life will have more
texture, color, and fun. You will be able to gauge other people's feelings better and understand your own. You can always
withdraw through choice back to the safety of First if under
extreme threat.

I'm leaving transformation with two quotations.

Most of our Third and First Circle defenses have been constructed through a fear of gravitas and a fear of joy, both of which lead to cynicism, which is the death cry of creativity.

> Cynicism is knowing the price of everything and the value of nothing.   —OSCAR WILDE

> The power of accurate observation is commonly called cynicism, by those who have not got it.
>   —GEORGE BERNARD SHAW

Power

> Nearly all men can stand adversity, but if you want to test a man's character, give him power.   —ABRAHAM LINCOLN

Power only tests the quality of our characters because its misuse is so very tempting. Consequently, we cease to empathize with other people's feelings, tolerate their ideas, or accept their rights and, at worst, their humanity. I am certain that the only way we can be equal in power with others is through Second Circle energy. Equal power, and meaningful, life-changing human connection and communication, happen when two people or a group of people are in Second Circle energy together.

When people are present with each other in Second Circle they are equal and in harmony, and this connection is the real definition of intimacy. Everyone in this energy is connected and transformed. Together in Second you see each other, know each other, and have a unique chance to understand each other's humanity.

> The meeting of two personalities is like the contact of two chemical substances: if there is any reaction, both are transformed.
>   —CARL JUNG

On the other hand, every destructive relationship, be it personal or professional, has an uneven distribution of power.

There is no shared experience or good use of power. One person is holding power over the other and the other is at that person's mercy: a condition that can easily engender shame in the inferior person. Of course, many people at some point hold positions of power. At work someone has to have responsibility of power over colleagues. Parents must take responsibility for their children, and the same applies for a teacher with students; but it is the use of this power that is crucial. Such power doesn't mean you cannot be equal in Second with those you are responsible for and who are in your care.

> Don't walk behind me, I may not lead. Don't walk in front of
> me, I may not follow. Just walk beside me and be my friend.
> —ALBERT CAMUS

The good use of power should be a daily practice for those with power, and if you believe you have more power than those around you, you will obviously have a greater struggle to be in Second with those "under" you. Parents might feel that their children are not equal and can be smacked. A teacher might believe that a student needs to be humiliated or a boss might wish to put work colleagues in their place or even bully them.

Beware if you fall into any of these categories—and to some extent we all have done so—because, as my grandmother said, "What goes around, comes around." Or, as Shakespeare more eloquently put it,

> . . . that we but teach
> Bloody instructions, which, being taught, return
> To plague th' inventor; this even handed justice
> Commends th' ingredients of our poison'd chalice
> To our own lips.

Macbeth is seeking a reason to murder King Duncan, a friend and a good man, and he realizes that the murder will return to plague him.

Socrates puts it another way:

> It is never right to do wrong or to requite wrong with wrong,
> or when we suffer evil to defend ourselves by doing evil in
> return.

This ancient wisdom is as relevant today and as potent now
as then.

As I have explained, Third Circle is a dehumanizing, brutal way
of power and control. Withdrawing your power into First is
passive-aggressive and can appear to be complicit, and this
includes hiding your head in the sand when you are witnessing the destruction of others around you. In Dante's *Inferno*,
those who are complicit have their own special place in hell for
this passive sin. This is because tyrants can only remain tyrants
when those around them turn a First Circle blind eye. The only
way to use your power is in Second Circle with those around
you. You and those reliant on your power will be more creative,
productive, and safer.

> They that have the pow'r to hurt and will do none,
> That do not do the thing they most do show,
> Who, moving others, are themselves as stone,
> Unmoved, cold, and to temptation slow,
> They rightly do inherit heaven's graces . . .
> —WILLIAM SHAKESPEARE, Sonnet 94

Gender

Equality between men and women has been a great obstacle
and struggle, a source of pain. To simplify this momentous and
ancient conflict, we have to accept that we are a mixture of the
physical and the emotional, the intellectual and the spiritual.

Any sensible woman understands that men have more physical force than most women. Of course, women have immense

physical power—childbearing and birth are an obvious example—but we know that an average man can physically overwhelm an average woman. Even though in extreme passion a woman can physically harm a man, she generally can't overwhelm him. This Third Circle force has led many men to the easy and smug conclusion that women are unequal in other ways—an argument that is flawed and ridiculous.

The puniest gorilla could outforce the strongest man, but that doesn't make gorillas a superior species. Women and men can outwit a gorilla and destroy its force in other ways. Men who feel superior to women wouldn't accept a gorilla's emotional, intellectual, and spiritual superiority over them, yet they still believe they are better than women and that women don't deserve Second Circle equality.

The long history of men assuming that their physical power means they have complete power over women makes the negotiation of power between the sexes today extremely difficult. Some men are so scared of women's power that they have created cultures that force women to be constantly in First Circle, if not completely hidden. The hijab, or head scarf, is an example of this—paradoxically, for women who are fearful of the unwanted attentions of men, First Circle and invisibility can feel liberating. Historically, women have suffered for their power through punishments ranging from ridicule to burning at the stake and stoning to death. This brings about a two-fold effect: women are compelled to retreat into First under the attack; and men are more likely to move up into Third Circle. This war can be resolved when men and women meet equally in Second Circle—not just sexually but emotionally, intellectually, and spiritually. The benefit to men will be as bountiful as the relief will be to women.

The Third Circle energy that men adopt makes many lonely, and intimate Second Circle contact hard. Most male-on-male contact is in Third. They might make Second Circle contact talking about sport, music, or sex, but in great emotional need they are not as capable as women of asking for help in Second Circle, particularly from other men. At least women gossip with each other and explore emotional pain together in Second, something that the men's movement is at last encouraging men to do.

Male energy moves toward Third Circle and female energy toward First Circle. As energy moves into Second Circle, the male-female mix in all of us neutralizes. We become closer to our psyches.

You can understand the Second Circle through an intellectual process, but to live in it and sustain it you will need to approach it through your whole being. You are not a brain on a stick; your presence is manifested throughout your body, breath, voice, words, mind, heart, and spirit.

5
Body

Opening Yourself to Second Circle

The word "body" conjures an idea of matter and substance. It is the main part of us. Sense and senses flow through our body and in this way energy unifies the body and is connected to it. That is, until you witness a dead body or even sit with someone as they die. Then you know that a body houses, but isn't, energy itself.

It is the housing of energy and the work you must do on your body that concerns us. A naturally placed body is present and correct in Second Circle. The body is centered and available. It is open and allows energy to pass through its matter, to give out and receive Second Circle energy back through itself. You were born with a connected body, but have probably lost the way and are now riddled with habits that block your present energy. These habits have disconnected you from your body and your body from the world; but Second Circle can remedy this.

Each part of your body has its own natural connections, but you begin to lose these when the parts of the body fall out with each other. The fallouts are the results of stress, tensions, blocks, unhealed injuries, and body blows gathered through the normal course of life. We all remember from childhood a song that goes, "the knee bone is connected to the thigh bone, the thigh bone is connected to the hip bone . . ." And so they are; but if you forget and lose these connections, you do so at your peril. You are misplacing your body and pulling yourself away from the life energy of Second Circle.

When the parts of your body are misplaced, this traps and distorts your energy. As the body's casing is pushed or pulled out of shape it becomes harder to be in Second Circle. Even if you manage to keep your energy, the world looks at you and sees distortion, not your real power. However, when physical survival is involved, even the most distorted body can rapidly rediscover its Second Circle natural self. Have you had any of these experiences?

As you fall, trip, or are propelled from a moving vehicle, your body has a strange sense of déjà vu with its natural and centered state—all distortions, tensions, and blocks melt in a fraction of a moment as you find your feet or roll out of danger.

Remember the strange dance you make as you save yourself from falling over in the street? This dance can cover a lot of ground and have you zigzagging in counterpoint for several seconds. Think of the relief as you find your footing and stand upright. Suddenly you are aware of how useful your feet are and of the contact they make with the earth. For several hours after, you can experience the wonder of a body working, and being centered and present.

Remember the physical joy of the dance performed privately to your favorite piece of music? How great, alive, and centered you feel afterwards. Or the moment you throw a ball perfectly or swing the golf club with brilliant abandon; the dive that has you entering the water with such ease and precision; the jump over a gate when you are being chased by a laughing friend. For some time after these activities you feel great in your body and it is often in this "great" state that you connect to the world with clarity. You see people and landscapes vividly. You have returned home to your centered presence, and that feels positive.

In this chapter you will relearn how to center and place your body naturally, giving you access to your physical presence and your real physical beauty. The physical beauty debate has always been a tricky one. I don't believe that you can be physically beautiful unless you are centered and present in your body, but the media has persuaded many that unhealthy distortion is preferable to a healthy, centered body.

The So-Called "Beautiful" Body versus the Natural, Centered, Healthy One

Many women, and increasingly more men, are distorting their bodies to fit an image that is unreal and unhealthy. In doing so, they pull their body into a constant First Circle state or push it into a rigid and hard Third Circle one. The pursuit of a cosmetic body shape is blocking present energy in millions of people. Some of us are born with aesthetically pleasing bodies, but nothing is served if you choose to cosmetically distort your body to fit an unreachable ideal that effectively disconnects you from yourself and others. The rich physical sensations of life—exercise and sex, for example—are actually dulled in a distorted body, as the divisions within the body disable it from wholly digesting the experience.

It always amazes me that in the so-called centers of physical beauty, such as Hollywood, the fashion world, the "cool" clubs of London and New York, you will observe the most contorted and destroyed bodies on the planet. These bodies couldn't survive and run away from a wild mouse, let alone a dog or a lion. They can hardly walk or stand, and yet they are considered beautiful. Such images of wrecked, unhealthy bodies are killing people: waifs who couldn't stand up in a gust of wind; bodies built up with so much hard muscle that they can hardly take breath; fashion shaping bodies into positions of complete submission.

A centered body deemed "ugly" by the cosmetic world is distinctly sexier than a distorted "beautiful" body. Just for a while, try not to judge yourself cosmetically but see your deep self and seek your body's natural beauty.

Here's a task for you: Try to look beyond the surface of yourself and others—the hair, the weight, the makeup, the teeth, and the clothes. See the *placing* of bodies.

Find and examine any recent photographs or videos of yourself. Preferably choose shots in which you are unaware of the camera so you have been less likely to control and "place" yourself. As you look at the images, blur your eyes so you can see the deeper shape of your body as opposed to the cosmetic outer effects.

- How comfortable do you look?
- How at ease are you?
- If other people are in the images, do they keep their space around you or are they taking your space?
- Are you mostly looking down, spine slumped, shoulders rounded?
- Do you have your chest lifted, your spine rigid, and your shoulders up?
- Are you pushing your head forward or pulling it back to look down on others?
- If standing, does your stance either diminish or exaggerate you, taking up too little or too much room? Are your feet together or too far apart?
- Are you centered, at ease, upright without lifting your upper chest, your head balanced, stance relaxed?

The answers may vary with the different images. The ease of Second Circle might be captured when certain people are around but not available to you when others are present. This is very useful information. Now rummage back through old photos and see if you can observe and mark changes in the placing and ease of your body. Acknowledge the changing shapes of the placement of your body. Don't try to understand them yet—we'll do that later.

Secondly, do some serious people-watching! Take time to do this both with strangers and with those you know personally and professionally. Begin to observe whether you shrink or brace yourself while watching. This will change, depending on who is present in the space with you. You might be able to watch in Second Circle ease if unnoticed, but this will probably change if you are observed observing. If you get caught up in the surface features of these people, blur your eyes to look deeper at their physical structures. You will begin to see very clearly those who shrink into First Circle body and those who take up more than their rightful space—Third Circle bodies.

When you observe a Second Circle, properly placed and aligned body, notice and sense its understated power, ease, confidence, and openness.

As you scan groups of people, ask yourself the following questions. Be honest, and have no shame about what you discover. Hiding from what you know is diminishing you. Your answers should coincide with the Circle types I have added to each question.

> *Who could I bully?* First Circle bodies can arouse in all of
> us a feeling of power, as they are usually life's pushovers.
> They are the people you could imagine taking on with-
> out much thought. Don't forget, though, that the world
> is packed with stories—many comic—of bullies mistaking
> someone who looks an obvious victim but is actually a
> black belt in karate! Or do First Circle victims arouse in you
> a need to protect them?
>
> *Whose presence can you not ignore?* Third Circle—but maybe
> it is because they are not trustworthy. Second Circle are
> equally hard to ignore but more approachable.

Who seems aggressive? Third Circle. Their bodies are braced
and looking for action.

Who seems not interested in others? First or Third Circle.

Who could you approach? Second Circle.

Who would help you if you needed assistance? Second Circle.

Who is sensitive? First Circle or Second Circle.

Who would you challenge? First Circle.

Who frightens you? Third Circle or the ease of Second Circle.

Who takes space with force? Third Circle.

Who doesn't take space? First Circle.

Who takes space with ease? Second Circle.

Who earns the physical respect of others? Second Circle.

Even after a short time spent assessing the shapes and energy
of people and groups, you will realize how much you already
know about the energies of others and how these energies
change you. As a general rule, those who take without giving
are First Circle; those who give out without taking are Third
Circle; and those who give and take equally are Second Circle.

As you realize what you already know subliminally about energies, you must accept what others know subconsciously about
your energy. This shared, subliminal human knowledge has shaped
every encounter of your life. You need to bring this understanding
into your consciousness and also to know that even if you believe
your body has lost its Second Circle energy, you have this energy
elsewhere. When you find your strong Second Circle place, you
will be able to transfer this place into other parts of yourself.

A sportsperson or dancer can be in Second Circle body but
unable to be there in other parts of themselves. A brilliant
scientist can be in Second Circle through their mind but not
their body. A passionate artist can be in Second emotionally
but in First or Third intellectually. When you understand your
strengths, you are able to work on your weaknesses.

Remembering the Natural Second Circle State

Remember the times you felt good in your body, unconscious of its "faults" or "wonders." Your body is an efficient, effortless instrument, housing you and making you aware, through its ease, of your own energy and the energy of the world around you:

Walking in nature on rough ground

On sand beside the sea

Riding a horse or bicycle

Gardening

Performing a repetitive but constructive physical task—housework can sometimes do this if you are not stressed or rushed

Stacking books, logs, etc.

Shoveling snow

A well-played physical game—particularly when it involves swings—tennis, golf, casting fishing lines or nets

A cartwheel, tumbling, a trampoline, a trapeze

In the physical presence of power—a horse or tiger

Breaking a brick in martial arts

Being in the presence of someone who doesn't threaten or judge you physically

Any of these activities generally will place your body back into its natural, Second Circle present state. In Shakespeare's *The Tempest*, Prince Ferdinand is set a physical task of heavy log carrying. This privileged young man is made to work physically until he realizes that work can be a source of delight.

There be some sports are painful, and their labour
Delight in them sets off.

You may want to seek out activities in order to return to your rightful physical presence.

Remember the relief and aliveness felt after a game of golf, the Sunday soccer game, the hard tennis match, the martial arts or yoga class. Of course, these activities increase the heart rate and oxygen intake, but they also replace the body into Second Circle presence. As you return to life after these activities, walking to your car or waiting for the bus, you notice how whole, complete, and present your body feels. This feeling lasts until you return to First or Third Circle habits.

Such physical aliveness and potency is one of the reasons why rituals are performed. Rituals prepare your body for the sacred and they release your energy, feelings, and thoughts. They open the body to receive wisdom and clarity and to release and purge negativity. When I was honored with a Tea Ceremony in Japan, I had to go on a ritualized journey which included crossing a river, walking on rough ground, and finding my way through a maze of pathways. By the time I was at the place of ceremony, I was physically ready to receive the honor. A well-conducted church service has the congregation standing, kneeling, even bowing—preparing for the miracle of the Eucharist in their bodies as well as their minds and spirits.

Ritual is so comforting and physically releasing that we all develop our own. Some can be compulsive. Families build their own rituals, as do cultures. The British make a cup of tea, which is an act of physical precision. This is done at points of crisis, not because people want tea and aren't feeling emotions, but because the ritual keeps you placed and present, not spinning out of control. Children love physical rituals to make them feel safe and centered: the toys placed in exact order; the story told with precision; the door ajar, as they sleep, but open to a very exact distance.

On my fourth birthday my sister Susan went missing. It was a perfect present for me as police and police dogs arrived at the house. I watched in excitement as search parties were dispatched. But, of course, for my mother it was a gathering night-mare and tragedy. To this day I remember my mother standing ironing with precision. It was her own ritual to stay centered and present in her body—she was bracing herself for the potential loss of her child. My sister was found unharmed and weeks of ironing had been done!

Now remember those you sought, or who sought you, that necessitated one or both of you being in physical Second Circle. This could be the smallest of shifts in your body.

Remember sitting with someone having a passionate debate, and how as the energy of the debate heats up, that surge of energy makes you first sit up and then even stand, centered and alive.

Remember love or lust across a crowded room, your body aligning with a stranger. Or maybe you stopped a stranger to ask the way and that stranger turned out to be the most Second Circle person available. And when you yourself have been asked the way by a stranger, the chances are you were in Second Circle or the most Second Circle person available on the street.

If you are harassed by a group in the street or a bar, you search for the most Second Circle person within the offend-ing group. This is the person with whom you might have suc-cess with a human appeal for mercy. Connected eye contact will draw both parties into Second Circle and the body will follow. Love, sympathy, curiosity, joy, and aggression all enter through your eyes into your body and leave again through the eyes.

Notice your body following your ears when you listen atten-tively to someone, and the reverse when you know someone is listening to you with similar attention. Remember Coleridge's Ancient Mariner:

It is an ancient Mariner,
And he stoppeth one of three . . .

He holds him with his glittering eye—
The Wedding-Guest stood still,
And listens like a three years' child:
The Mariner hath his will.

Now remember some of the events that distorted your body in the first place. It is impossible to travel any distance in life without someone disliking us or wishing to hurt and humiliate us, and our body is an immediate target. You might have had physical injuries that are still held in your body. These will include wounds, operations, and physical injuries that have pulled your body away because of pain. The act of acknowledging the body's wounds will help you to dismiss them. Now list the comments, events, or words that are still embedded in your body: the ones that have taken you out of Second Circle body and made you either shrink away (First) or push yourself tenaciously into the world (Third).

All negative comments about your body have a destructive effect on your physical presence. "You're fat, clumsy, ungainly, lumpen," will have spun you into First. "You're skinny or weak" will push you further into First or challenge you into Third. The bullied either retreat further into First or become Third Circle bullies themselves. Falls, accidents, physical pain, unless addressed, can take bodies out of Second Circle. Unwanted praise for your body or parts of your body, given by those who are abusive and unwelcome predators, can shift the body out of its presence. If this desire and abuse reaches its vilest mode—sexual abuse or rape—then a body retreats into a place of not being. You might even leave your body: the final form of First Circle.

6

Working on the Second Circle Body

The Second Circle body is a body with natural placement. Your energy moves through your body with ease and authenticity. The body is open and the energy of the world enters. This body is strong yet flexible, efficient in standing, walking, and running. It is not an underdeveloped, underused body that squashes and traps your life energy within itself. Neither is it an overdeveloped, muscled, and braced body that pushes energy into Third Circle. Rigid and held bodies are not open to the impulses of life.

Exercises: The First Stages

Wear loose clothing and no shoes. Stand in the most comfortable way you know and go through this checklist.

Feet. Are both feet on the floor, almost parallel and under your hips? If they are wider than your hips, you are in Third. If they are narrower, you are in First.

If the feet are not fully on the earth, then you are denying your presence and are in First. If they are too firmly planted and you feel it is an effort to get going off the ground and move with any spontaneity, you are in Third Circle.

- Your feet should feel and be engaged with the earth.
- Now shift your weight slightly forward on the balls of your feet, with your ankles released so that you could spring in any direction at any time.
- Your first substantial movement into Second Circle physical energy will be as you move very slightly forward on the balls of your feet but keep your heels engaged on the floor.
- Do this and you will begin to feel more alert and on your toes. More ready for life. If your habit is to stand back on your heels, you are placing yourself in First. This physical reduction in your energy might have forced you to push up into Third Circle.

Knees. It is unnatural to lock your knees, so check them. They should feel soft and not locked—if they are tense, then unlock them.

Knee tension pulls you into First, blocks the breath and voice, and can force you into Third Circle if you need to move out of a static, locked position.

Hips. Check that your hips aren't thrust forward, as this actually pulls you backward.

Pelvic thrusters are normally in Third Circle. The pelvis locks and forces you up into the rigid push of Third.

Spine. Where is your spine? If it is slumped and depressed, you are in First. If it is too rigid and held up, you are in Third.

- Sit on the edge of a chair with your feet on the floor. Feel your energy through the balls of your feet.
- Gently rock to feel the base of your spine.
- Slump the spine (First).
- Then pull it up too far (Third).
- Do this several times. You will begin to feel, as you pass

through it, the natural spine position—between First and
Third—a placing of ease that is the healthy spine.

- Now stand and feel the difference.
- You should begin to feel more in your body. The spine feels
  connected to your pelvis, knees, into your feet and the ground.

Shoulders. Where are your shoulders? If they are pulled back
or lifted, you are in Third Circle. If they are rounded, you are in
First Circle.

Your shoulders should hang freely, without a depression in
the upper chest (First) or a lift there (Third).

- Gently lift, drop, and circle the shoulders.
  After these movements let the shoulders go and find their
  own position. Don't control or attempt to place them. If
  you do this, you are putting them back into tension.
- Take one arm and gently swing it as though you were
  throwing a ball underarm.
  After several rotations, let the arm and shoulder find their
  natural position. The release will be immediate, with this
  shoulder noticeably lower then the unswung one. Repeat
  on the other side.
- As the shoulders find their rightful position, you should
  begin to feel the upper chest release. Remember to breathe—
  the breath will not only feel calmer but will also begin to
  enter the body deeper.

Head position. Is your head balanced at the top of your spine
(which ends behind your ears)?

Your head could be tucked in or looking down, on one side,
quizzically (First). It could be pulled back to look down on the
world, or jutting forward to penetrate it (Third). (Incidentally,
these positions will create neck and shoulder aches.)

In Second Circle the head is evenly balanced on top of the

spine, giving you a clear and undistorted view of the world. The
head can then move with ease.

- Let your head fall onto your chest and gently massage
  your neck.
- Allow your head to swing easily from one side to the other;
  then, after a few swings, let it come to rest on
  your chest.
- Shut your eyes and lift your head up until you feel it balanced on the top of your spine and connected to it.
- Open your eyes and check if you are seeing the world from
  a new position.
- During all the exercises for the head, keep the teeth
  unclenched—the lips together but the jaw free.

Now do a full check

- Feet—energy forward on the balls with heels also on the floor
- Knees—unlocked
- Hips—not thrust forward
- Spine—up, not slumped or rigidly held
- Shoulders—released, not rounded or lifted and pulled back
- Head—balanced, with ease, on top of the spine
- Jaw—unclenched, with the lips lightly touching

You must repeat this check after the next exercise below,
which is designed to center and align your body further.

- Stand slightly on the balls of your feet with your knees
  unlocked. Let your head fall onto your chest and its weight
  flop you over from the waist. Feel like a puppet hanging down from your hips. Shake out your shoulders with
  released knees and spine. Let your head go. Hang, and
  remember to breathe deeply.
- Stay on the balls of your feet and gradually come up
  through the spine. Let your shoulders fall into place at the

end of the movement. As you come up, don't push your hips forward or hoist your chest up.

- When you are upright, gently rock forward and back on your feet. If you are centered, you will balance and not stagger over.

- Play with your usual stance and rock. Notice if you feel less secure and balanced. Keep checking from your feet to your head and notice any energy shifts that try to pull your energy into First or Third.

- Stand in the centered position. Swing your arms up so you end up reaching for the sky, but without hoisting or lifting your shoulders or upper chest. Breathe calmly and silently.

- Slowly allow your arms to open to your sides assuming the da Vinci "balanced man" pose. Feel energy moving through your arms and out of your fingers. Release your shoulders and breathe. Allow the arms to return to your sides.

- *This is the most important moment.* As the arms return, you will feel either a need to slump the spine and depress the rest of your body, pulling you into First Circle—a clear sign you are a First Circle body—or a desire to brace the chest and spine up, into Third Circle. Fight these desires and you will feel open, strong, and available within your body. You will begin to experience a different flow of energy.

These exercises need to be repeated every day until you feel more in your body and available to a Second Circle energy.

You have now performed exercises preparing your body to feel the Second Circle. These next exercises will initiate a real Second Circle physical connection.

Activating a Second Circle Connection

- Walk, with energy and purpose, as though you have to go somewhere urgently. Breathe easily and look around you. Notice, even quickly, details in the space. Feel the earth through your whole feet. Keep the ankles released.

- When you feel energized in your body, come to a standstill but don't try to brace or lock your body. You are effectively still but not stopped. Energy is suspended.

- Check that you don't pull back on your heels, lock your knees, pelvis, or spine, or interfere with your shoulders. Don't jut your head forward, look down, or pull it back.

- Look around the space. See it clearly in this physical state. You should feel alive and alert.

- Feel energy through your back. The whole space around you feels available. You know and feel what's going on around you. This is bound to feel vulnerable to both First and Third Circle, so where you want to place your physical energy—withdrawing it (First) or forcing it out (Third)—is a good guideline to your habits.

- Repeat. Notice if you want to really stroll and scuff on the floor (First), or strive and make noise with your feet (Third). Second Circle is as silent as possible. To survive you don't want predators to hear you.

Try to walk with purpose but with efficiency for thirty seconds before stopping. See and experience the space specifically.

- Now move from walking into running, back into walking, then into standing and holding present Second Circle energy. Don't sink back or brace yourself as you come to stillness. You are fluid and alert; metaphorically, your ears are pricked up and the center of your body is tuned to the world.

- Run or walk quickly up a set of stairs, then stop and focus around you.

- How do you sit?

  A slumped position indicates First Circle.

  A rigid and exaggerated "good" posture is Third: shoulders back and spine hard.

  Make sure your feet are on the floor, shoulders released and spine effortlessly up. Rock to feel the base of your spine.

  Now get up with as little effort as possible, your head leading you, and walk as though you have somewhere to go. Come back and sit with all that walking energy in you.

  You will find yourself sitting with greater alignment. More energized. More present.

- Push with both hands against a wall. Look and focus your eyes onto the wall. Keep the shoulders free and chest open, your knees unlocked, and the balls of your feet engaged on the floor.

  Breathe easily and feel the breath low in your body. Your stomach should move outwards. Gently push yourself away from the wall and stand and look around you. Feel your presence. Repeat at least seven times.

- Remember the western saloon doors in cowboy movies? They represent a perfect Second Circle physical exercise.

  To push through them and arrive with dignity into the bar, you have to be in Second Circle. Any exaggerated, overdone attacking energy (Third) will propel the doors back onto you—deeply humiliating. Any underfocused, indirect, apologetic energy (First) will move the doors unevenly and produce a clumsy entrance into the bar.

Second energy is clear, direct and efficient. In the absence of saloon doors, you can experiment along the same lines through revolving doors. You know you are in Second if you can negotiate revolving doors with complete dignity of entrance and exit. Or line up two substantial chairs back-to-back on an uncarpeted floor and push through them. When you move through them with ease, you are in touch with Second Circle energy.

What you have started to feel is that if your energy is too relaxed or casual, the body falls into First Circle, and if it is too tense, controlling, or overexpectant, it will pull itself up in Third.

Additional Exercises

Here is a great exercise to do if you have an hour to spare and want to feel open enough to Second Circle energy. It is also great to do before you go to bed. You will sleep better and be better placed for Second Circle in the morning. I will return to this exercise later with additions to help you clean bad energy out of your being.

People in Third Circle will find this hard as they may feel powerless and frustrated. Those in First Circle will find the first section easy but the reengagement more difficult.

- Lie on your back on the floor in a comfortable, safe room. You shouldn't feel that you could be disturbed. Place your head on a thin book or cushion. Lift your knees up so that your feet are on the floor. Shake your thighs free. Gently lift and drop your shoulders until you feel them free. Then let your arms and hands relax.
- Place one hand on your upper chest until you feel it release. Place a hand on your stomach to help release any tension. Keep breathing as calmly as you can.
- Try to stay there for at least 10 minutes—more if you can bear it. Then slowly get up: roll onto your side, then onto your hands and knees. Roll up through your spine until you are centered. Check feet, knees, hips, spine, shoulders, and jaw. They and you will feel more released and placed.
- Most people will now be in First Circle, so go to a wall and gently push against it. Feel the breath low. Push yourself away effortlessly and you will find yourself in Second Circle.

Daily Practices and Exercises for the Second Circle

Actors, dancers, sportspeople, or anyone practicing a craft already know the power and fundamental importance of repetition. It is through repetition that work lodges into your body. I always say to artists that you have to know the work so well in order to forget it and live the work freely and forever.

So, don't be frightened of doing basic exercises in order to reengage to your natural Second Circle, the energy you were born to own.

One other observation. Our education system is heavily weighted in favor of the intellectual rather than the experiential. This focus encourages your mind to interfere with your physical energy. The mind can place you back in tension rather than living in the freedom these exercises offer.

Learn to be kind and non-judgmental toward yourself and allow yourself to play. Know that your mind is fine so it needn't overpower you. If you can't structure daily exercises for your Second Circle bodywork, try to incorporate these daily practices and activities into your life.

- Walk with clear, uncluttered energy, with focus and purpose. Notice objects, buildings, and so on, around you.
- If you spy a revolving door, go through it in Second Circle.
- Walk with purpose up any stairs, and as you reach your destination, stand and check your body and energy.
- Take every opportunity to walk in nature and on unpaved surfaces.
- If you have to spend hours sitting, take a brisk walk around inside or outside the building every two hours, and return to feel the different energy when you sit.
- Do the same after leaving your car.
- Stay attentive in meetings by keeping your feet on the floor and your spine up. Gently push against a table when bored and you will breathe lower and stay more present.

- Shake hands with Second Circle energy. Use a firm hand-shake with eye contact, not the limp First Circle handshake or the too strong, controlling Third Circle one.
- Enter spaces and rooms with Second Circle energy and purpose.

Within days you will have a new physical approach to the world and it to you. Take time to observe the world around you in the context of this energy.

- See the physical shifts of babies and children. Watch how their bodies fill with Second Circle energy as they notice a new toy or a wonder of nature like a bird or an insect. Feel and see their bodies turn off when they are bored and fall into First Circle.
- Notice someone slumped on a sofa in First, who suddenly gets an idea and sits up into Second Circle energy.
- Watch a sportsperson focus, like a tennis player winning shots in Second Circle. Notice how if they lose concentration—maybe because of a contested line call—they might push into Third Circle and lose more points because of their loss of Second. Between games they might sit in First contemplating their game plan; then, as they walk onto the court, they get up again into Second Circle.
- You might be able to spot that a footballer is going to miss an extra point if he is trying too hard to prepare for the shot in Third Circle.
- Athletes pace in First, reserving energy for the race, and move into Second as they wait under starter's orders. Those who move into Third are likely to have a false start.
- All great actors, dancers, and musicians move into Second before they perform.
- In meetings, you will sense those gearing up to ask a question in Second Circle. Even sitting next to or in front of the person, you can feel this shift of energy.

- Notice how some people can control meetings or class-rooms with generalized Third Circle energy, but fail to engage you.
- First Circle in public is always boring and uninspiring.
- Notice the physical energy of your family. Do you copy the energy or have you revolted against it? Imagine a Third Circle parent producing a First Circle child, or a First Circle parent's passivity forcing their child into Third Circle.

7

Breath

All human energy is breath. The body houses you and breath powers you. It's the first act you perform and it is the last. Breath powers your body, your voice, your mind, your heart, and your spirit. In fact, if you examine words like "inspiration" and "respiration," you notice the presence of spirit embedded in the word.

As you breathe in ideas, you touch inspiration, and on your last breath, you expire. Breath is the key to all your energy and is completely fundamental to being present. Most people take breathing for granted and most—in Western urban living—have ceased to breathe naturally, fully, or freely.

Every inhalation takes in energy from the world and attaches you to it. On exhalation, you send what is inside you out into the world, and in so doing you touch and change the world with your breath. Whatever is good or ill within us, in the connection to ourselves and the world, is clearly reflected in how we breathe.

If you have tied yourself in knots physically, then your breath is equally contorted. You have lost pleasure in taking breath and forgotten how important breath is. Watch how a baby releases distress through breath. The last shudder of a bout of crying enables the baby to move forward from anxiety into comfort and it comes to rest with the next breath.

How Do You Breathe?

Consider the following questions:

Where do you feel physical movement in your body as you breathe?

Do you regularly hold your breath?

Can you hear your breath?

How often are you aware of your breath, either in panic or in joy?

Are there people who affect your breath? Do they either stop you breathing or enhance your breath?

Are there situations when you know your breath will fail you?

Are there environments that block your breath?

If you have been able to answer any of these questions, you already know a great deal about your breath and its habitual problems.

Try to monitor your breath over a few days to get a clearer knowledge of its strengths and weaknesses, and then return to these crucial questions. Examine each question and explore with me the consequences and meanings of your answers.

Where Do You Feel Physical Movement in Your Body as You Breathe?

Here is a physical description of how your breath should work naturally. As you inhale, there is no lift in the upper chest or shoulders, but you can feel an opening through the sides and back of the rib cage. (Perhaps the last memory you have of this natural movement is after a good laugh: "I laughed until my sides ached.") Half a second to a second after the rib cage opens, there is release and movement down through the stomach and abdominal muscles, into the groin. When the inhalation is complete, there is a fraction of a second when the body feels suspended and ready (the suspended readiness you feel before throwing a ball, jumping, or letting out a free cry or laugh).

The natural inhalation takes enough air to live, move, think, feel, or express what is needed and is appropriate at that present moment in time. This natural breath completely serves every present need without blocks or holds. You take enough: not too little and not too much. Every part of you is satisfied with this natural breath.

Natural exhalation is when the muscles that have opened out (ribs) and down (abdominal) move in to create a column of air that releases your energy into the world—be it thoughts, feelings, movements, or words. On exhalation, the spine, chest, and shoulders shouldn't collapse or tighten. You shouldn't feel any constriction by breathing or squeezing out too far. After that moment of easy suspension you take a new, calm breath into the body, rib cage widening, abdominal muscles moving out and down.

When the outward breath focuses on a specific point, you are immediately in Second Circle and connected to that point through your breath in a very tangible and powerful way. Your energy touches that place, person, or object.

If you breathe in this natural way, you are already very present and powerful. You are aware of the world around you and see it clearly. Your power has already been recognized and your presence felt.

Unfortunately, most of us have lost this natural breath and experience different and often blocked physical movements with inspiration and exhalation. The work in this chapter is to rediscover the natural breath that marries to your presence. It can only be positive to breathe naturally and equally; any unnatural patterns of breath can only produce negative effects in you and the people around you.

- Do you feel a shallow breath—one that is high in the body?
- Do you breathe with your shoulders lifting or rounding, your chest collapsing?
- Is there little or no movement in your rib cage or abdominal area?
- Do you hear sighs as you breathe?
- Is your breath taking up little space in your body? On the exhale is there little to give out?
- Is your body squeezed, in order to exert any energy into the world?
- Is there so little oxygen in you that even small amounts of stress panic the breath?

If you have answered "yes" to three or more of these questions, then you are a First Circle breather.

- Do you feel a large lifting or hold in your chest as you inhale?
- Is your rib cage tight, forced, and locked as you breathe in?
- Are your shoulders pulled back and the back of your rib cage arched?
- Is the whole process one of overstretching and forced expansion?
- On exhalation, do you force the air out and hear your breath as you then draw it in?

If you have answered "yes" to two or more of these questions, then you are in Third Circle.

Do You Regularly Hold Your Breath?

It is natural to hold your breath for a moment if you are shocked or require a sudden shift in your attention; but this hold should not continue beyond the event. If you regularly hold your breath, you do not want to be noticed and probably desire to blend into your environment. Breath has to have movement, and by stopping that movement you are avoiding being present and seen in the world. You are rather like a mouse aware of a hawk hovering overhead. This stillness is a survival tactic, but the mouse reengages its breath after the hawk has gone. This is clearly First Circle breathing.

If you breathe in and hold a breath in an overexpanded and lifted body, you are trying to keep as large as possible, for as long as possible. You are imposing your full size onto the world. This is most definitely a Third Circle breath.

Can You Hear Your Breath?

Again, the occasional inward gasp or outward sigh is natural if it is connected to an appropriate need. For instance, an unexpected event will produce a gasp and a need to release follows the unexpected with a sigh. Noisy breath is only problematic when it is habitual and regular.

Third Circle breathers inhale with noise to impose their presence on the world as the sound of their breath signals that they are about to speak. First Circle breathers sigh out, giving away power and communicating weakness, even sadness or despondency. However, if you are present in the world, aware of your surroundings, and desire survival, a silent breath is natural. You don't want predators hearing where you are.

How Often Are You Aware of Your Breath?

A natural breath is silent and effortless; only noticed when the exertion or emotion passing through your body is greater than normal emotions or your fitness level. First Circle breathers are often aware of panic and stress in their breath and they fear situations that demand more oxygen in case they lose control. Third Circle breathers feel that they need to overcontrol their breath, so they hold and force it. This breath is rarely organic to emotions and thoughts and may have force but not fluidity.

Are There People Who Affect Your Breath?

Generally, Second Circle breathers will make any of us feel safer than First or Third Circle breathers. Sometimes their breath presence can change our patterns, bringing an unnatural breath into its natural place.

A First Circle breather will feel very intimidated by a Third Circle one and can shrink further into First in that person's presence. Two First Circle breathers together might feel safer, but the space between them fills with a deenergized vacuum.

A Third Circle breather might not even notice a First Circle one or at worst might feel a temptation to bully him or her. Two Third Circle breathers risk a face-off and clash of presences.

When you have learned to breathe naturally in Second Circle, you begin to energize the First Circle breathers around you and disarm the Third Circle ones.

Are There Situations When You Know Your Breath Will Fail You?

When you are in touch with your Second Circle breath, you will be able to troubleshoot any sense of impending breath failure, which can include panics or locks.

If you know your breath can stop or diminish, this is a sign of First Circle breathing. Overcontrolling the breath when panicked is Third Circle breathing. Try to remember a situation that frightened or disturbed you and reexperience what your breath did then.

First Circle breathers dread any public event when they have to be on show, so that going to a party can produce a panic breath, as can speaking in public. Third Circle breathers may feel uneasy in intimate exchanges, particularly hearing ideas or experiencing emotions that they have no sympathy with or control over.

Are There Environments That Block Your Breath?

It is possible that even the thought of certain spaces can throw your breath into panic and holds. For instance, the memory of certain meals, classrooms, people, elevators, traffic jams, trains, and so on, sends shockwaves through your body. If you do remember these shocks, it can help you to understand your breath and the constant fears that impair your breathing.

Most people on this planet are now urban dwellers, which doesn't help us find our natural breath. Our breath works better in nature. It is where we started and probably where we belong.

Have you noticed how your breathing can miraculously regulate itself when you are looking at the sea, mountains, woods, a sunrise or sunset, or up at the stars? As you breathe with nature in Second Circle, you connect with nature and can even start to feel at home and at ease. This connection applies to hostile terrains and, actually most vividly, in powerful weather. A strong wind will knock you off your feet unless you breathe naturally with it. If you have ever experienced being on a boat in a storm or swimming in rough seas, you know what I mean. Your breath had to stay in connection to your environment or you would drown.

The more we all lose a connection to nature, and the more we are crammed into small spaces with low ceilings and dwindling daylight, the more most of us shrink into a First Circle breath, or try to push away and break out of the restricting surroundings with a Third Circle breath.

In fact, I believe that space and oxygen on the planet lessen as more humans compete for dwindling supplies of clean air, so you have to practice Second Circle breath consciously. I passionately encourage you to take any opportunity to sit and breathe in nature and place yourself in large and epic spaces. Even a visit to a local park or cathedral can open up your breath to its full and glorious potential.

I think if you examine these basic questions again, you will really know whether your breath is in First Circle with the life force being sucked out of you on a disturbingly regular basis, or whether you have all the controls of Third Circle breath that, at worst, can take oxygen from those around you. Please don't blame yourself, as all of the habits that destroy us or others have been learned, acquired in order to survive the humiliations of life. However, these are the consequences of First and Third Circle habits, and this is how these habits are perceived by the people around you.

First Circle Breath

With this breath, you might be perceived as a victim, ineffectual or weak—it makes it hard to connect to the outside world and easy to be overlooked and ignored.

We all need First Circle breath to reflect and commune with ourselves; but if we want to be present in the world and at ease with our families and communities, it can only be an unproductive breath.

Third Circle Breath

With this breath, you will tend to be overnoticed and at worst can be considered overbearing—a bully, controlling, insensitive, and arrogant. People are rarely at complete ease in the company of a Third Circle breather.

Initially, this is a breath energy that can appear impressive, creating a surface enthusiasm in others. Eventually, it dehumanizes others as they feel powerless around you. People will either want to attack you or leave you.

We all need the occasional Third Circle breath when we cannot afford to engage with someone, or in a situation such as an uninvited intrusion; but if we stay in Third Circle with our family and communities, we risk their feeling unimportant and redundant in our presence.

Exercising the Natural Breath

Below are some exercises that will help you to reencounter your natural and Second Circle breath. Try to do them for a few minutes every day until the natural breath stays with you. You should also do these exercises before important occasions in your life.

You can do the work by daily monitoring of your breath, but it is important that you work with as much subtle awareness as possible. This subtlety will help you negotiate tiny nuances and changes in your breath patterns, which will give you enormous insights into your power, passions, and fears. Remember that every thought and feeling manifests physically, first in the breath, so its regulation is continuous and a life journey. Simply, breath work continues until your last breath is completed and you finally let go!

I started to study breath when I was nine. The work consisted of learning techniques of breath control for stage and speech exams. Over the course of many years I took exams in breath and passed many with distinction.

At nineteen, I went to the Central School of Speech and Drama in London, at the time the finest training for breath and voice in the world. After leaving Central, I started teaching breath and voice for up to sixty hours a week. My technique was good, but deep down I knew I hadn't taken a proper Second Circle breath in years.

When I was twenty-nine, I left a very destructive relationship. At three o'clock in the morning, standing in a London square looking up at the stars, I felt my first natural Second Circle breath in years. Twenty years after the beginning of my quest, I touched my present breath. And the work continues.

So, be patient; work with kindness toward yourself. Don't be frightened of tears. It is all right to cry, and when you do feel your full breath power, you have the right to that power.

The Two Stages of Breathing

The work has two stages:

Inhaling and allowing the breath to widen and deepen your body.

Exhaling, then allowing the muscles of breath to support the release of your air and energy.

Inhaling

- Stand centered in the ready body position, the energy of your body slightly forward on the balls of your feet. Your knees should be unlocked, your spine up—not slumped or too held and rigid—and your shoulders should be released and hanging free.
- Walk around the room with purpose to feel Second Circle physical energy. Breathe.
- When you stand still, don't brace your body and stop your energy. Keep breathing.
- Now flop over to one side keeping upright (be careful not to lean forward). Allow the arm on the stretched side of the body to arch over your head, with the other arm hanging free. Then silently and calmly breathe. You will start to feel

the rib cage stretch on the arched area—increase this stretch through the rib cage, pull on the arched arm that is over your head, and continue to breathe.

- As you stand up, that stretched side will feel wider and open with a much deeper breath entering that side of your body. You might begin to feel a release in the abdominal muscles, just above the groin. This is very good.
- Keep checking that the shoulders and upper chest aren't lifting. Repeat this stretch on the other side.

The second exercise is a bigger stretch of the breath into the body, particularly into the back of the rib cage and the lower and abdominal muscles.

- Hug yourself, wrapping your arms close to your chest, but keeping the shoulders free.
- Now take a slightly wider stance by unlocking your knees further by a few inches.
- Still hugging yourself firmly but with free shoulders, flop forward from the waist and keep your neck loose. Calmly breathe in and out at least seven times. You will feel the back of your rib cage open and energy move down through your spine and into your backside. Eventually, you will feel the lower muscles release into the groin.
- After these breaths, let your arms release and hang forward. Now come up slowly through your spine, letting your shoulders fall into place with your head coming up last. Be careful as you will feel a bit dizzy, but you will be aware of a deep and powerful breath settling low in your body.

This exercise is very effective in placing your breath. It is also helpful to try before stressful events. It will always calm and empower you.

At this point you have opened up the sides and back of your rib cage with these powerful inhalations. Now you need to concentrate on your lower breath. As you do this next stage, keep the upper chest still so that you avoid its lifting or depressing and the ribs swinging.

- Take a stance with your feet placed at about the width of your shoulders. Bend your knees as deeply as you can, but keep your feet on the floor and your spine upright. Place a hand just above your groin and feel the breath release those lower muscles as you calmly and silently breathe.
- After seven breaths, stand up and keep the breath low. This breath will take time, so don't rush the breathing.
- An overall stretch of these muscles can be obtained through yoga's "child's pose": Get onto your hands and knees and place a small cushion or piece of thick material under your feet and knees. Don't tighten your thighs together.
- Collapse your backside back onto your feet, allowing your head to go to the floor, with your arms stretched out in front of you and your shoulders and thighs released.
- Now breathe slowly to engage all the breath muscles of the body.

  Please don't continue this exercise if the position hurts your knees or spine—I don't want you in pain! If you can't bear it, sit up and go back onto your feet, keeping your shoulders free and the spine up.
- Suddenly and easily your breath will drop into place, very low into your body. You will feel its enormous power and this can scare you or make you emotional, but do please persevere.

Exhaling and Support

The next two stages are exhaling and support. Breathing this deeply and freely into your body enables you to identify the moment when your breath is suspended. This suspension isn't a lock or hold, which would take you into Third, and it isn't rushed, which would be First Circle. It is you breathing as and when you need to and honoring the present moment before you act. This creates a moment of readiness in your breath and in you. Such readiness is one of the greatest physical sensations of power you will ever feel. When you use this sensation, it will give you your rightful presence and Second Circle connection to yourself. You begin to be present *to yourself.*

The whole process of inhaling and suspending the breath, ready for the power of the exhale, works very well with swinging motions. Swinging is not only good for the breath but is a good way of describing the action of breath.

- Imagine throwing a ball underarm. Inhale as you swing your arm back. Your arm will suspend with the natural suspension of your breath, and as you throw the imaginary ball, your arm moves forward with exhalation and the breath throws the ball.

- This breath supports the projection of the ball, your voice, or a movement. The support projects you and everything in you out to the world. It effectively connects you to the world, and in this way becomes Second Circle breath.

- Try a First Circle throw. Let us stay with the image of throwing the ball. Breathe in, with your arm swinging back to throw the ball, but throw it before you feel suspended and before the breath is ready. You are throwing without any power leaving you, so you are unable to connect to the world.

- Now try a Third Circle throw. Breathe in, drawing your arm back. Feel the suspension but lock it so that there is no fluidity or readiness—the resulting throw is one of force and overcontrol.

- Return to the Second Circle throw. Swing back with the breath in, feel the suspension and readiness of the breath,

and release on a supported *sss* sound. Do this until you feel
the breath is synchronized with the sound.

- Try using this method to throw a ball against a wall or to
  swing a weight with the breath. After a few minutes, the
  breath and sound will come together. The breath underneath supports your energy.

The next stage is to feel the moment you run out of breath
and support, and when you need to inhale.

- With the natural breath you will feel this moment as a clear
  desire to breathe in and gather new support, and you will
  take the next breath calmly. This will not be a snatched
  First Circle breath or the overdrawn, forced inhalation of
  Third Circle breathing.
- On exhalation, you should not feel that the outward
  breath support fades away and gives up. This, of course,
  is First Circle exhalation. Third exhalation is too determined to push through the release. In these ways, First
  Circle has little or no support and Third Circle has too
  much support.

Here is another way to feel readiness of support. It is a simple
pushing exercise.

- Place one or two hands against a wall, then exert a little
  pressure on the wall. Keep your shoulders and upper chest
  free and unlocked, with your weight on the balls of your
  feet and your heels on the ground.
- Maintain this pushing pressure and breathe in and out
  calmly. The breath should be low and you will feel a synchronized breath and support as you push.
  In this way you will feel when you are losing support
  and need to inhale. This inhalation will come easily if the
  breath is silent and low in the body.

- When you come away from the wall, you will feel more connected to your breath, yourself, and the world.

This free and flexible breath places you in the moment and can then serve your physical, emotional, and intellectual needs.

The more you breathe naturally, the more present you will be.

8

Second Circle Breath: Reaching Out

Here are some simple reminders. You are ready to reach out to the world in Second Circle.

To connect to and touch anyone or anything in the world in Second Circle, you have to breathe to them. Literally, your breath touches them.

First Circle breathers only go some of the way to their point of attention as their breath is falling short of the target. On the other hand, Third Circle breathers send their breath beyond and through the target. First is too little. Third is too much.

If you want to command and hold a space and have the right to be there in any space, you must breathe the *complete* space in Second Circle. Breathing to half the space leaves you in First. Breathing beyond the space places your energy into Third.

Intimacy with another human being is an equal exchange of air with and to each other through the placing of the Second Circle breath. First and Third Circle breaths have no intimacy. First is not reaching out enough to the person. Third is over-reaching through and even flattening the person.

Here are the basic exercises for placing your breath and being into Second Circle.

- Place your hand in front of your face, about a foot away. Look and fully concentrate on your hand and breathe to it. You will feel the moment the breath touches and connects to your hand. You are now touching your hand in Second Circle.

- Breathe half the distance to your hand and you will feel immediately closed down into First.

- Now breathe past your hand and you will feel the extra distance and your energy shift into Third Circle.

- Now take further and longer connections. Travel longer distances with your breath. Find a point across the room. Breathe to it. Feel that connection. You will be taking more breath but are still connected to yourself and to that point.

- First Circle will find the breath dropping off before it reaches that point.

- Third Circle will find you breathing beyond the room, maybe even drilling through the wall.

- Now breathe the whole room with the connected Second Circle. When you feel this, you are in command of the entire room. All great performers and speakers breathe the whole space they are in. They don't breathe half the room or overbreathe it, as this disengages them and they would lose their charisma.

- If you breathe in all the rooms you have to work in, and all the new rooms you enter, your easy power will be palpable.

- As you enter a party, you will feel in control and less afraid.

- If you breathe the space as you enter a room for an interview or presentation, you will be immediately more impressive and less daunted by an audience.

- The next time you pet a friendly dog, remember to breathe to it. Not only will you notice the dog but the dog will notice you and it will obey you more readily.

- Children are very responsive to this breath as you get their

attention more effectively. They will listen to you sooner
and calm down faster.

The next time a work colleague ignores or irritates you,
breathe to them and notice their shift in energy. Shake hands
and breathe to the person and they will register you sooner and
even remember your name better.

You will begin to notice that you can draw a First or Third
person's energy into Second if you breathe to them.

Daily Applications

Start to notice the world around you differently through your
body and breath in Second Circle.

Notice the people who you can make Second Circle contact
with and how that fully engages you to them for good or
ill. Even if it lasts for a second, it is tangible. Notice those
who are less able to make this contact with you.

First or Third Circle people cannot easily notice others'
engagement as their own is shut down or overblown and
desensitized. Hence, they will blunder into intimate Second
Circle connections without being aware of their intrusion.

Consciously notice how lonely you feel when someone with-
draws their Second Circle breath connection to you. We can
remember this abandonment years later.

Observe couples in First. Restaurants are good venues to
notice this detachment: two people dining together but
actually alone.

A bad presentation has First Circle breath. Teachers, man-
agers, and actors can make the most interesting material
boring by a delivery in First Circle breath. A presentation in Third Circle breath might keep our attention purely
by its force but rarely imparts information. You might be
impressed but you don't learn.

Notice how breath patterns can be contagious. It will take
you some effort to maintain Second Circle breath when the
most powerful person in the room is in First or Third. A
leader can infect their family and work colleagues by their
energy patterns. The depression of First breath is catching
and unchallenging, and the force of Third breath makes a
challenge hard to mount.

A nervous performer in First Circle panic breath causes the
audience to breathe with the same unease. A pumped-up
Third Circle performer can overstimulate an audience with
his or her generalized energy.

A Third Circle bully looks for a First Circle breather to
victimize.

A therapist draws you out with Second Circle breath, as does
a skilled interrogator or salesperson.

Try the following techniques:

• Breathe to the people who serve you—waiters, taxi drivers,
sales assistants—you will find you get noticed sooner and
receive better service.

• Breathe to a child in distress—it will help calm them and
give them security.

• Breathe to the other person on important telephone calls—
you will immediately gain more authority.

• Before any presentation, go into the room and mark the
space with your breath. Feel how much breath you need to
present in that room. The bigger the space, the more breath
you will need.

• Listen to people with a Second Circle breath—you will hear
them more accurately.

• Breathe to the road around you as you drive—your driving
will improve.

• Breathe to someone as you give them a compliment—it will
enter them more deeply.

- Woo in Second Circle body and breath—you will be more successful in your dates.
- Breathe in interviews across the desk—you will appear more attractive and human.
- Breathe through fear in Second Circle. Even if you can't face a person directly, imagine breathing into them—the fear of them will loosen its grip on you.
- Breathe into places that have scared you in the past—a cloud will lift.

The body houses the breath. The breath powers the voice.

9

Voice

If you bring forth that which is within you, that which is within you will save you. If you don't bring forth that which is within you, that which is within you will destroy you.

—The Gospel of St. Thomas,
Gnostic Gospels, no. 70

The sound, availability, and focus of the human voice really matter to all of us, particularly at crucial points in life. In moments of crisis, when the voice of another human touches us, it can either help or hinder our survival, or guide us through distress and pain. At these moments we hope for a voice that touches us with care, that is direct, clear, free, and connected to us.

This, of course, is the Second Circle voice. When communication is important, none of us wants words mumbled incoherently in the fashion of First Circle. Who needs a doctor telling us bad news in a First or Third Circle voice? Or a priest speaking at the funeral of a loved one in a detached or overcontrolling way? In failure or difficulty, you don't want to be vocally patronized, ignored, shamed, or sentimentalized. By now you can probably identify which of the above descriptions fall into First or Third Circle voice.

You don't want any of these, but you also don't want to come across in any of these ways yourself; you care about the person or people you are communicating with.

Sadly, the tensions in your body, breath, and voice can convey negativity, carelessness, and insensitivity, even if your heart and mind desire to sound compassionate and caring. The natural voice is free and responds authentically to the feelings and thoughts we are experiencing in present moments of our life. It is built and designed to reach out and touch others in Second Circle.

Your natural voice sounds as you really mean to sound, and, equally crucial, the function of a free voice and sound is to purge your body, heart, and mind of pain. This purging can only work when you release your voice fully and freely. A good cry, laugh, or curse only serves you if you let sound and voice out freely, not swallowing it in First Circle or pushing the release forcibly in Third. A Second Circle voice makes you feel better.

When your voice forms words, the words connect you and your experience to the world. By voicing and speaking words to the world, you are known and witnessed by the world. You can only be known and heard and your life witnessed when you use your voice and words in Second Circle.

Anthropologically, it is posited that free voices developed to make the complex and tribal sounds that bind communities together. It is true that the free voice is a powerful social force and tool. After all, you meet your community and are safe within it if you speak to and with each other. At that point, as you share your stories, you create your histories together.

Apes are instructive to us. They groom every individual in their family group each morning. This is a way of checking that everyone is all right and that all in the community are present and correct. Historically, as groups got larger, this grooming would have taken all day, so, as one theory goes, speech developed so that one could say, "Hello, how are you?" instead.

This simple but important exchange is universal in all families and workplaces, but it is not effective unless you are speaking and responding in Second Circle voice. We are lost in our families and communities when this essential check doesn't happen or is performed in First or Third. We are potentially in terrible jeopardy if this human exchange that is built into our human DNA, ingrained over tens of thousands of years, fades, or doesn't happen at all in our daily life, or is manufactured, losing all intimacy by being in either First or Third Circle voice.

Remember, your voice is the most immediate way of communicating complex information about yourself or others, and the voice's health and quality are dependent on the body. Unnatural tensions anywhere in the body reduce and constrict the sounds your voice can make. Further, the voice's power and variety are totally reliant on breath and support—without sufficient breath, your voice becomes underpowered and First Circle. With too much tension and effort in your breath support, you push your voice and it becomes Third Circle.

You know how effective voices can be, either positively or negatively. Voices will either turn you off or engage you enough to listen.

The First Circle voice disengages the listener and actually does the same for the speaker. It is a voice that deenergizes everyone around it. It is difficult to hear, dull and lacking in range; it has a downward, often pessimistic fall, and as it trails away it can depress both speaker and listener. A First Circle voice asks the listener to move toward it, so that the listener has to do all the work in understanding what is being said. It is a mumbled, swallowed, or whispered sound, which can create a growing desire for us to yell, "Speak up!"

The Third Circle voice will turn you off because it is pushed. The listener may actually feel the pain of a pushed voice in their own throat. The listener feels flattened because there is no flexibility in the voice. It can be too loud and persistent, if not aggressive. It can be too controlled or manufactured. Third Circle voices sometimes try to sound beautiful—a frequently mesmerizing affectation that hides meaning.

Other Third Circle qualities can be described as controlling, arrogant, aloof, uncaring, dominant, even too enthusiastic or jolly. All this provokes in the listener a simple desire to yell, "Shut up!"

The positive voice—the one that is effective—compels us to listen and touches us freely.

The Second Circle Voice

Here is a list of Second Circle, natural voice qualities:

It cares about reaching the listener and is generous in touching you.

It is a flexible voice, which reflects what is being said and reveals rather than hides content.

It is an interesting voice, and recognizes the listener's presence by being neither too soft nor too loud.

It is an effortless, vulnerable, clear, and intelligent voice, which has an immediate impact on the world.

It is a voice that encourages the listener to think, "Go on."

I want to tell you about the voice you were born with, the free voice that calls out with the certain expectation of being heard and answered. This is your unique, vigorous, healthy, and wondrous voice, that has for many of you been knocked, squeezed, ripped out, or hidden within you. I believe that somewhere you have a memory of this marvelous voice: a memory of ease and joy as you spoke, laughed, or indeed wept.

Maybe this voice came when you had a clear knowledge that you were thrilling the listener and your words were effective and active in them, like those times when you told a great story and gained appreciation or applause. Or maybe your need to communicate was so powerful that you became superarticulate and utterly uninvolved with yourself and what others thought of you, because you had a genuine need to speak and affect others. Then, your voice was tireless and full of variety. It was the voice that expressed you in the present moment and made you and your audience present.

You have to trust that you still have this voice. It can be recovered and exercised with daily work and commitment. Let us now investigate your habits—I think you will find that these questions give you a clear idea of what Circle your voice is in.

- When you speak, do you notice people leaning into you (First) or backing away? Third.
- Are you asked to repeat yourself? First.
- Do you feel you force people to listen? Third.
- Do you give up or trail off sentences? First.
- Do you think that volume will control the listener? Third.
- Do you find yourself droning on (First) or manufacturing your voice to be more interesting? Third.
- Are you aware of people tuning out when you speak? (This last point can be true in either First or Third voices.)

Generally, a First Circle speaker is more aware of failures than a Third Circle one. This is because Third Circle speakers can be so busy controlling others that they miss an audience's reaction. It goes over their heads.

Now answer these questions about any physical sensations around your voice. They will be even more relevant after public presentations, a couple of hours of constant use, or when you are nervous.

- Does your voice ever hurt? (A sure sign of pushing in Third.)
- Does your voice tire easily? (Can mean a Third Circle pusher or a First Circle whisperer.)
- Is it hard to feel the articulation in your mouth—particularly your lips and tongue? (You are a First Circle mumbler or swallower of voice.)
- Does your head jut forward as you speak? Third. Or do you look down? First.
- Do you clench your teeth and therefore your jaw? Third.

• Do you feel a lump in your throat? (This could be First Circle holding or a Third Circle pusher.)

You have begun to assess how you sound to others and how your voice feels to yourself. Test yourself by recording and then listening to yourself speaking this poem by Samuel Taylor Coleridge. I completely understand that most people hate listening to themselves, but this is an important exercise and step if you can bear to do it.

> A damsel with a dulcimer
> In a vision I once saw:
> It was an Abyssinian maid,
> And on her dulcimer she played,
> Singing of Mount Abora.
> Could I revive within me
> Her symphony and song,
> To such a deep delight 'twould win me,
> That with music loud and long,
> I would build that dome in air,
> That sunny dome! those caves of ice!
> And all who heard should see them there,
> And all should cry, Beware! Beware!
> His flashing eyes, his floating hair!
> Weave a circle round him thrice,
> And close your eyes with holy dread,
> For he on honey-dew hath fed,
> And drunk the milk of Paradise.
> —SAMUEL TAYLOR COLERIDGE, *"Kubla Khan"*

Next, use a tape recorder talk for at least thirty seconds about an aspect of your life. By speaking a poem and then talking about yourself, you will be speaking first formally and then informally.

After the recording, wait a day—this will give you some objectivity—then play back and analyze your voice, using the descriptions I have provided. What I really hope you will hear and identify are any holds or vocal tensions, and the exact quality of energy your voice has. Please bear in mind that you are going to shift these tensions and recover your natural, free voice.

If you are habitually a First Circle speaker, this work is likely to make you feel too loud and committed. Any Third Circle speaker will probably feel underpowered, less effective, out of control and vulnerable. However, the freeing will make your voice feel more flexible and effortless, and it will begin to make a better impression on those around you.

Freeing the Voice: Second Circle Voice Exercise

Throughout this exercise, be sure to

- Sit or stand centered, with a constant reference to Second Circle bodywork.
- Breathe low and wide into the rib cage and abdominal muscles. Constantly support the voice with a fluid Second Circle breath sent out to a point in the space.
- Breathe throughout with the ready breath always underneath the sound.
- Gently massage the face, particularly between the eyes, beside the ears, and around the hinges of the jaw.
- Bunch up the whole facial mask and hold this position for 7 seconds before releasing the muscles. Allow the muscles to return to the position they want to go into, not the ones you want to place them in! Repeat at least three times. Your face and jaw should feel more open—the jaw less tight.

Start this exercise with your lips together but your teeth apart.

- Slowly begin to smile, and as the smile widens, open the jaw as far as you can without any discomfort or force. Keep the smile in place—don't let it droop. This movement will automatically open the throat—the fundamental prerequisite for a free voice. This opening may be accompanied by a desire to yawn, but the yawn is a good sign as it indicates the throat has been opened. Do this five times.

- Next time you do this exercise, silently breathe in and out when you release the jaw. You will experience a deep connection down through your body to your lower abdominal breath. This connection can only occur if the throat is open. There should be no rasping of air in the throat—this is how the throat should always feel when you are vocalizing and speaking.

- Now speak with good breath support on the edge of a yawn. Although this sounds strange it immediately stretches tension out of the throat and begins to free the voice. Experiment with this famous poem by William Blake:

Tyger! Tyger! burning bright
In the forests of the night,
What immortal hand or eye
Could frame thy fearful symmetry?

In what distant deeps or skies
Burnt the fire of thine eyes?
On what wings dare he aspire?
What the hand, dare seize the fire?

And what shoulder, & what art,
Could twist the sinews of thy heart?
And when thy heart began to beat,
What dread hand? & what dread feet?

What the hammer? what the chain?
In what furnace was thy brain?
What the anvil? what dread grasp
Dare its deadly terrors clasp?

When the stars threw down their spears,
And water'd heaven with their tears,
Did he smile his work to see?
Did he who made the Lamb make thee?

Tyger! Tyger! burning bright
In the forests of the night,
What immortal hand or eye
Dare frame thy fearful symmetry?

- Now speak, just thinking of a yawn, and you will begin to feel a free voice.
- After this stretch, let the lips come back together, with the teeth and jaw unclenched and the throat ungripped.
- Breathe in calmly, without noise, through the nose, and begin to hum gently. When you run out of breath, breathe in and start again.
- Hum until you feel your voice vocalize without stickiness or spluttering. It should feel effortless. If it doesn't, you are trying too hard (Third).
- Hum different notes with ease.
- Place your hand on your head and hum—you should feel a buzz in your forehead or even your head.
- Hum into your nose.
- Hum into your face and aim to get vibration on the lips.
- Hum as smoothly as possible down through the range.
- Repeat this last part three times.

Now your voice should feel warm, freer, and fuller; but it is probably still held inside you in First Circle, so you must try to place your voice deliberately into Second Circle. If you are a Third Circle voice, be very aware not to push during the next exercises.

Placing the Voice in Second

Next, you need to reach out with your voice.

- Find a point across the room just above your eyeline. Breathe to that point, maybe even imagining throwing a dart on the breath to target the point.

- A free-placed voice moves up and out of you and should not rest in your body. Place your lips forward as though you are going to speak an *oo*. Send air through that position, feeling the breath support and its readiness without vocalizing.

- Now actually sustain an *oo* to that point. Try to avoid the sound falling off and dropping back into you (First) or forcing the voice (Third). Imagine throwing a dart as you vocalize to this point. Release an *oo* at least three times.

- The next step is to move from an *oo* to an *ah*: *oooahh. Ah* is a very open and vulnerable sound, so you might find yourself pushing for it (Third) or pulling it back into you (First).

- Send the sound with an underarm throw or try imagining throwing a net out to sea as you release.

- If you find yourself pushing, think of a yawn just before vocalizing.

- If you find yourself falling off the sound, use one hand and push firmly but gently against a wall as you release the sound. As long as the shoulder remains released and the breath low, this physical push will help you monitor the sustained placing of the voice. The push makes you feel clearly when you drop off the sound.

The next exercise, called intoning, is one of the most wonderful and effective exercises for your voice as long as it is done with breath and freedom. It will build up the voice's freedom, strength, and fluidity. Doing it, you will "get on" your voice, away from whispering, and feel immediately when you use throat tension to push it.

- Intoning is a sustained release of voice on one note, rather like a monotone chant. Intone this phrase: "The grey sea and the long black land" to a point above eyeline. Throw or push it if required.

- Repeat the phrase at least three times.

- Now start intoning the words and on the same breath move into speaking.

This could take several attempts to achieve, but once done you will experience a free, powerful, and placed voice.

Now take the whole poem, not just the first line.

The grey sea and the long black land;
And the yellow half-moon large and low;
And the startled little waves that leap
In fiery ringlets from their sleep,
As I gain the cove with pushing prow,
And quench its speed i' the slushy sand.

Then a mile of warm sea-scented beach;
Three fields to cross till a farm appears;
A tap at the pane, the quick sharp scratch
And blue spurt of a lighted match,
And a voice less loud, thro' its joys and fears,
Than the two hearts beating each to each!

     —ROBERT BROWNING, *"Meeting at Night"*

- Intone it all, and before you have time to consider the exercise or your voice, go straight into speaking the poem. Then repeat.
- Re-record the Samuel Taylor Coleridge poem on page 81. This time, breathe to the tape recorder and imagine you are speaking to a good friend, someone who is supportive of you and on your side. Keep the voice free and forward. Feel the freedom of the jaw and space in your throat and mouth.

On listening back, you should hear more movement and color in your voice. You should be able to hear and concentrate on the words rather than the sound you make. The words should be reaching you with less effort.

Daily Workout

- Spend 10 minutes in the morning checking your body and breath, and vocally warm up and place your voice. Finish up with intoning into speaking.
- Make an effort to speak freely and clearly to someone on ten occasions during the day—maybe shop assistants, receptionists, waiters—and on the telephone to people who don't know you.
- When you feel more comfortable using your voice, try it out on people you know but who belong to the outer circle of your life, such as neighbors, casual friends, colleagues you know but don't work closely with, or people you are starting a relationship with at work or personally.

As your confidence grows, you should feel able to connect freely with the inner circle of people you know; they may ridicule you, but don't let them stop your growth.

Over the days and weeks of your vocal experiments, you will notice that reactions to your speaking have changed for the better. A First Circle communicator will feel more noticed and heard. A Third Circle communicator will notice a greater ease in the voice, and will sense less fear, maybe even sympathy, from others.

You should now take a pause and assess what you have worked on and accomplished. You have exercises and techniques that can place your body, breath, and voice into present connection to your world. Even if you don't read on further and merely do this first stage work, your life will be transformed and your presence will be felt more powerfully and humanely. You will feel better and more alive on a daily basis, and know when you need to troubleshoot parts of your body, breath, or voice if you are knocked out of your Second Circle presence by life's unwholesome forces. In this pause you should appreciate what you have achieved and that this work is fundamental to the next stage of Second Circle awareness.

From here onward, the work deepens. In some senses it becomes more interesting, but equally it is more difficult.

The work you have done so far can be rationally understood and clearly felt; but as we progress, it will become less concrete and, to some people, more problematic.

Many of us are educated to bow to the god of rationalism and suspect the imagination. Think about this: If your heart is broken, you know it's cracked though an X-ray might show nothing at all.

As the work deepens, so does the learning. I do completely believe that long-term learning is only possible in Second Circle. Your mind can only be set free when a teacher teaches in Second Circle and the student learns there. A Chinese proverb says that "Teachers open the door. You enter by yourself."

Let me remind you how ancient crafts were—and in some cases still are—taught. The apprentice watches the teacher, his or her attention on everything the teacher does. The student only asks questions when he can perform certain processes. Without active participation, the student cannot learn or perform the work or understand its relevance. Learning requires full attention before you perform any skill; but once you can perform and understand the skill, you have learned it forever.

Learning is not compulsory . . . neither is survival.
                                                    —W. Edwards Deming

10

Words

Suit the action to the word, the
word to the action.

—WILLIAM SHAKESPEARE, *Hamlet*

When you have worked on your body, breath, and voice, you are
ready to work on your speech and words.

The articulation of a word—speech—is the final physical act
in the chain of communication. This chain starts, as you now
know, in your body, and is powered by your breath and given
voice by the vibration of your vocal folds. Then your voice
enters your mouth, is articulated by your lips and tongue, and
molded into the word. The word passes through and out of your
mouth into the world. The word has been yours, but as it leaves
you, it belongs to others, and is present and alive in them and
in the world.

A Second Circle word leaves your mouth, travels on your
breath, and enters and touches its target. If you speak in First
Circle, your voice falls backwards into you so you are unable
to fully articulate the word—voice energy is being pulled or is
falling back and away from your lips and tongue. This means
you consequently mumble, and can't complete the word, so it
becomes depressed and distorted. You might feel the power of
language and try to engage words in Second Circle, but this
power and energy is being locked in you. Words and expression
fall into the past, and even joyful words sound depressed.

In Third Circle speaking, the words are pushed out with force and sometimes overarticulated, so that even when there is a deep connection in you to the words, they sound shallow and insincere. The words are pushed into the future and even gentle words sound aggressive.

Words cannot sound present if they are not allowed to live in the world or are being pushed past it. As I hinted before, First Circle words live in the past and Third Circle words live in the future. If you mean what you say as you say it and then send it forth, you are speaking in Second Circle.

Language

Words touch you. Your words touch others. The words spoken by you or to you are still living. They live in another or in you. They are bedded in bodies, minds, and hearts, be they tender or violent words, insults or praise.

Remember when your words changed someone else: the way they looked at you, heard you, and reacted to you? In those remembered moments, the word was given and received in Second Circle, and therefore transformed your world for good or bad. Now acknowledge what your words do or could do when given and received in Second Circle.

This Second Circle exchange is the most profound experience you can have with the spoken word. When it happens to you, you realize that the old saying, "Sticks and stones will break my bones but words can never hurt me," is *wrong*. The physical power and energy of a word spoken in Second and entering you in Second Circle is fully meant by the speaker and will be unforgettable to the receiver.

Let's take those three little words: "I love you." If you speak these words in First Circle, they fall back into you and you are speaking them to yourself. The object of your affection might hear the words, but the words' true energy is being pulled back into the speaker—you. Perhaps you are too frightened of committing in Second Circle or you are actually saying, "I love myself"!

If you speak those words in Third Circle, they are pushed into the world generally, without landing specifically on your beloved. The receiver could be anyone—you are either bluffing, fearful of commitment, or saying the words to shut the receiver up!

A First Circle or Third Circle receiver wouldn't notice this lack of clear focus, but a Second Circle receiver will feel disappointment. Deliver them in Second Circle and you have to stand by the words, as they now exist out of you, in space. You have given words form and life, and they are alive and concrete. In this way, Second Circle words are meant and are therefore transforming.

Try saying the word "no." In First Circle, it falls back into you. You are reprimanding yourself. In Third Circle, it is generally not aimed at a target. Only in Second Circle is it a direct "no" to someone, clear, defined, and meant.

Here is a silly experiment but it does illustrate the point. Say "Sit" to a dog in First or Third Circle. Normally, a dog will not respond; but in Second Circle, the dog sits. A young child responds to Second Circle but can easily ignore you when addressed in First or Third. This is because animals and children know and live the power of Second Circle connection through sound. They know this—and really we all suspect it. This is why at the heart of all sacred practices lives the knowledge that a prayer, spell, or curse has the potential to change, create, or form the world. But only when delivered in Second Circle.

A word only has power when delivered and received in Second Circle. But the word must be meant and appropriate to Second Circle, because each circle of energy has its own native vocabulary.

The language of internal, personal monologue comes from the First Circle. The language of intimacy that is meant for someone outside you is Second Circle language. And then there is the language of public pronouncement, which lacks intimate connection to the world, and is obviously Third Circle. Although each language is appropriate in its context, importing the vocabulary of one Circle into another is confusing and jarring to listeners, leaving them wondering how to take what you are saying.

When the Second Circle language of intimacy is delivered in Third Circle, it feels intrusive, insincere, even threatening. For instance, service professionals like receptionists and flight attendants have all been trained to speak to customers in Second Circle language. "Have a nice day," "How are you?" "Are you all right?" These caring and intimate phrases are frequently delivered in Third Circle because they can't be intimate with four hundred people a day; but the inappropriate delivery of Second Circle language deadens the words and actually debases them.

Drunks are frightening or at best boring because they speak First Circle language—the words and references that only they understand—with a Second Circle delivery. They know what they are talking about and can get enraged that you cannot crack their personal language; and because drunks can't listen in Second Circle, they are lost to you and to themselves. A mentally distressed person on the subway disturbs you in the same way. First Circle words, that you have no way of deciphering, penetrate you in Second Circle.

So the tasks at hand include:

Delivering words in Second Circle

Meaning what you say, as you say it

Knowing that your fully engaged words delivered in Second Circle change people and the energy of the world around you

Being aware that no one will hear what you mean unless they are in Second Circle. You will learn not to waste important words when the person you want to communicate with isn't in Second Circle. Remember the miserable experience of delivering important words in Second Circle to someone who is in either First or Third Circle—the height of being misunderstood!

Sound Equals Sense

When you release a word in Second Circle, you experience its full physical form and sound. This sound releases a word's sense. In Second Circle, you have the power to project the word's full potency.

Physical Exercises to Connect You to Second Circle Words

- Warm up your body, breath, and voice.
- Walk with energy, and as you come to a standstill, keep that energy in your body. Feel the floor through the balls of your feet.
- Look around the room, making Second Circle eye contact with several objects. Note how alert you feel. Check that you are not pushing your body into Third or retreating into First.
- Breathe low and feel the readiness of the breath support. If you don't feel it, either imagine throwing a ball underarm or gently push against a wall.
- Find a point of focus just above your eyeline.
- Breathe to the point.
- Send an *oo* to the point.
- Allow the sound to leave you effortlessly without force (Third) and without falling back into you (First).

When you feel that the sound connects to the point, maintain that connection as you read aloud one or all of the follow-

ing sonnets printed below: Elizabeth Barrett Browning's "How
Do I Love Thee?" (No. 43 of her *Sonnets from the Portuguese*);
John Donne's "Batter My Heart"; and Shakespeare's Sonnet 57,
"Being Your Slave."

> How do I love thee? Let me count the ways.
> I love thee to the depth and breadth and height
> My soul can reach, when feeling out of sight
> For the ends of Being and ideal Grace.
> I love thee to the level of everyday's
> Most quiet need, by sun and candlelight.
> I love thee freely, as men strive for Right;
> I love thee purely, as they turn from Praise.
> I love thee with the passion put to use
> In my old griefs, and with my childhood's faith.
> I love thee with a love I seemed to lose
> With my lost saints—I love thee with the breath,
> Smiles, tears, of all my life!—and, if God choose,
> I shall but love thee better after death.

Elizabeth Barrett Browning's poem starts with a direct question, which is then answered as a list. The poet's soul reaches to
the end of her being in love. She is present to herself and gives
that presence to her lover, through day and night, purely, passionately, with breath, smiles, tears, and beyond. The language
is present and intimate—Second Circle—and her love given in
Second Circle.

John Donne, on the other hand, is talking directly to God,
and the shock is that the language to God is violent. He asks
God to ravish him and break the marriage he has with the devil.
It is a direct appeal to the sacred.

> Batter my heart, three-person'd God; for you
> As yet but knock, breathe, shine, and seek to mend;
> That I may rise and stand, o'erthrow me, and bend
> Your force to break, blow, burn, and make me new.
> I, like a usurped town, to' another due,

Labour to admit you, but O, to no end;
Reason, your viceroy in me, me should defend,
But is captiv'd, and proves weak or untrue.
Yet dearly I love you, and would be loved fain,
But am betrothed unto your enemy;
Divorce me, untie or break that knot again;
Take me to you, imprison me, for I,
Except you enthrall me, never shall be free,
Nor ever chaste, except you ravish me.

Finally, a "slave" confronts a lover. Within this direct confrontation are moments when Shakespeare tries to appease his lover for having been so controversial, direct, and in Second Circle with his needs.

Being your slave, what should I do but tend
Upon the hours and times of your desire?
I have no precious time at all to spend,
Nor services to do, till you require.
Nor dare I chide the world-without-end hour
Whilst I, my sovereign, watch the clock for you,
Nor think the bitterness of absence sour
When you have bid your servant once adieu.
Nor dare I question with my jealous thought
Where you may be, or your affairs suppose,
But, like a sad slave, stay and think of nought
Save where you are how happy you make those.
    So true a fool is love that in your will,
    Though you do any thing, he thinks no ill.

All three sonnets are addressed to someone, and therefore the language is Second Circle. "How Do I Love Thee?" is an expression of love to someone; "Batter My Heart" is directed to God; and "Being Your Slave" is a direct challenge to a lover to whom the writer is bound as a slave.

The language of poetry should always be in Second Circle; it would distort the language's power to speak it in First or Third, and be pointless to speak it to someone who isn't listening in Second Circle.

Try speaking one of these poems in First and then in Third. Notice how First renders the language powerless and Third makes the language shallow. Both readings lack a trust in the words and the ideas expressed in them; in fact, when not delivered in Second Circle, the language becomes redundant as it does not match the energy it was written in. Now return to being in Second with the poem and speak it. Communicating these great passions in Second Circle is hard, but the language and words should feel appropriate when delivered in this way.

Connecting Your Words to the World

- Still focusing and breathing to a point above your eyeline, just speak the vowels of a poem. You will feel the sounds forward in your mouth and even some of the emotions the vowels release as you voice them.

- Now add the consonants, making sure each one is firmly but gently articulated. Feel the word and contact it in your mouth before you let it go. If the word is not fully defined, you are pulling it back into First. If it is too defined, you are controlling it in Third.

- As you do these exercises in Second, you might experience how the consonants give physical meaning to the words. "Batter My Heart" has many sounds of violence in it. "How Do I Love Thee?" feels loving, and is firm and opinionated as well as powerless. "Being Your Slave" is full of anxiety, waiting, and rage.

As you read these poems, you might come across words that you, personally, find difficult to say. Maybe you find it hard to express love, address God with such clarity to show rage, or be clear with your opinions. When this happens, you will either pull into First or push into Third to prevent yourself facing those words.

- Take a line or phrase and build it up in this way:

  How
  How do
  How do I
  How do I love
  How do I love thee?

- Focus each word in Second Circle to a point of focus outside you. If you manage to stay in Second, you are really beginning to touch the world with words.

- Now try speaking the next series of words in Second Circle:
  "I wonder . . . mmm . . . maybe . . . perhaps I'll go shopping later . . . what would he like as a present? . . . I'll think about it later."

  Obviously, there might be words in that ramble that pop out in Second, but most of the words are inappropriate to Second Circle.

First Circle language is a conversation with yourself constructed of words and references that only you understand, and they can help you negotiate yourself around a problem. They are not words for the rest of the world. Your inner world is known to you and doesn't need certain explanations. When you deliver First Circle language in Second, at best you aren't understood, at worst you're considered disturbed.

Try these sentences in Second:

"Will the owner of the white BMW that is blocking the sidewalk please contact the front desk."

"Passengers are reminded to keep their luggage with them at all times."

These public announcements might sound strangely intimate in Second because the language is general and suits Third Circle. Now try them in Third Circle and feel how the words begin to fit.

Language fitting the Circle is what constitutes appropriate communication. When this occurs in your own speech, you are clear about your intentions, and you might then experience how difficult it is to receive communications in Second Circle. Obviously, this is true when unpleasant things are spoken to us, but it can also be true when positive words are rejected by the receiver. If that has ever happened to you, you know how dispiriting it is. Imagine the disappointment of gathering all your energy to say something gorgeous to someone who then refuses to accept it in Second!

Later in the book we will work on ways of bringing people into Second Circle, so that you can deliver important words when the person you need to hear those words is ready for them.

Imaginative Language Exercises

The physical exercises should have given you sound and form connection in Second Circle, and that should have started to connect you to the sense of the word. Now we can go further and explore the imaginative engagement with words that will make their release in Second Circle more revealing.

If the word is to reveal itself fully in Second Circle, you have to fully imagine it and know it in your body, breath, mind, and heart, so that each word is made concrete. In the exercise below, you will have to enter the word by going into First Circle and own the word inside you in order to place it in Second Circle, outside you.

- Lie on your back with your legs up—feet on the floor.
  Breathe low into the body. Wait for the breath to be ready.
  Shut your eyes.

- Take a series of words that have powerful meanings and imagine each word, making it concrete and alive. Don't speak the word until you have an experience—be it visual, sensual, a memory, or a feeling.
- When you first speak the word, it will be in First Circle.
- Open your eyes, breathe, and place the word into Second Circle. The word is now fleshed, has blood flowing through it, and lives. Work with these words: *life, death, love, hate, all, nothing, depth, breadth, tempest, guide, worth, batter, heart, knock, seek, town, star, lips, error.*
- Now do the same with a list of sayings:

My heart is broken

I am falling in love

I will stand my ground

These are my rights

- As you experience words and speak them, you mean what you say. When your language sounds trivial or superficial, it is either because the language *is* trivial or because you are not experiencing or meaning it as you speak it.
- Try speaking one of the poems quoted earlier, experiencing and concretely imagining every word. This takes time but is very rewarding.

Now speak one of the poems in Second Circle. You will find that you now know parts of the poem as you have started to learn it by heart and experience!

Speak what we feel, not what we ought to say.
          —WILLIAM SHAKESPEARE, *King Lear*

- As a daily practice, read aloud in Second Circle: information manuals, newspapers, etc.; you will immediately know the material better and have learned it deeper. Speed and skim reading are done in Third Circle.
- Try to write from First into Second Circle—your writing will have extra power.

- Think of the words that have changed you.
- Think of the words that have changed the world.

Read some more words aloud in Second Circle. Here are a few examples that may help:

To no one will we deny or delay right or justice.

No free man shall be taken or imprisoned or deprived or outlawed or exiled or in any way ruined, nor will we go or send against him, except by the lawful judgment of his peers or by the laws of the land.   —MAGNA CARTA, 1215

. . . We hold these truths to be self-evident, that all men are created equal. . . .   —DECLARATION OF INDEPENDENCE, 1776

I have the heart and stomach of a king.   —ELIZABETH I

The most positive men are the most credulous.
                              —ALEXANDER POPE

So long as the great majority of men are not deprived of either property or honour, they are satisfied.
                              —NICCOLÒ MACHIAVELLI

These powerful words would not have resonance if they were not delivered in Second Circle voice and powered by Second Circle breath through a Second Circle body.

11

Listening

Like speaking, good listening is an acquired skill. Even if you have anatomically perfect hearing, you may not have been listening to other people. Unless you listen in Second Circle, you do not hear properly.

Some people hurt themselves by listening in First or Third Circle. We might appear to be taking in sounds and information, yet actually what is heard is filtered through our subjectivity. When we listen in Third Circle, we scarcely hear at all; we are so busy pushing our own presence out that we mishear everything around us.

First and Third Circle listening can be dangerous and leave us powerless in the world. We don't hear the sounds or words that will help survival; but in the moments when we have to survive, we do hear and listen in a clear and vivid Second Circle. You hear in Second Circle the small, strange sound that alerts you that something is amiss in your home or the quality of a footfall that confirms you are being followed. As parents, we can identify and respond to our child's cry even in the cacophony of the playground. We recognize the laugh across a crowded room that confirms our lover has arrived at the party. My "deaf" grandmother could hear very well when she realized we were discussing her!

These examples prove you can be shocked into Second Circle

listening and that your ear has the constant potential to hear extremely well. Imagine what you will hear when you work on listening in Second Circle.

In ancient Greek history, there is a story that highlights Second Circle listening. During the Peloponnesian War, a whole fleet of Athenian ships was destroyed by the Sicilians and many Greek soldiers were taken as slaves to work in the silver mines, which was a terrible fate. As it turned out, the Sicilians loved theatre, particularly the plays of Euripides, and if a Greek slave could recite a section of a Euripedian play, the Sicilians gave the slave his freedom. Now, these plays of Euripides, we believe, were only performed once, so you had to be there at that performance, and most of the captured soldiers were not educated to read or write. They heard the play once and remembered some or all of the text. These recollections eventually gave them freedom. That is Second Circle listening.

There is a similar example of this attentive listening in Shakespeare's *Hamlet*. Hamlet asks an actor to recite a speech he heard once: "I heard thee speak me a speech once, but it was never acted; or, if it was, not above once." Hamlet then proceeds to remember thirteen lines of the speech.

I used to have doubts about these two stories until I worked with students who couldn't read or write but who did listen with fiery attentiveness. These oral students could learn a text on one hearing.

If you need to hear, you listen in Second Circle. If you need to learn but can't write to retain knowledge, you listen in Second Circle. Second Circle listening will not only improve your chances of survival but also improve your relationships personally and at work. You will become more attractive to everyone you meet. People who listen in Second Circle are wonderful to have in your life.

No one likes to be called a bad listener, so when it is suggested that you are not listening, either you get defensive (Third

Circle reaction) or sulk (First Circle). We all desire to be listened to in Second Circle as this is a human need, so let's practice returning the favor.

All of this is hard, as we live in a very noisy and rushed world and rarely experience silence and stillness. Without this experience of silence, urban dwellers in fact find it hard to hear. Consider the questions below and formulate your own responses. I have numbered the points for easy reference later when I answer them myself.

How Do You Listen?

1. When did you last hear only nature—and did it frighten you?
2. Who is the last person you really listened to?
3. Who was the last person who really listened to you?
4. List the people who never listen to you.
5. List the people you never listen to.
6. What was the content of the last news report you heard?
7. What did you discuss with your partner yesterday?
8. What did you discuss at work yesterday?
9. What was the last piece of music you heard that stays with you?
10. When did you last hear music that moved you?
11. How often do you think you've missed information?
12. How often do you interrupt?
13. How often do you assume you know what's coming up in a conversation?
14. How often do you need to hear simple instructions before understanding them?
15. When did you last hear words that changed you?
16. When did you last hear a voice that affected you?
17. When was the last time you were seduced by someone listening to you, or vice versa?
18. Who listened to you as a child?

I know this may be making you uncomfortable or even sad, but go on and get active. Read the questions aloud with your body in Second Circle and with the regular low breath and free-placed voice of Second Circle.

Like speech, listening is an extension of the breath. When you listen properly, you do it through the breath. Sounds and words flow through your breath and touch you, just as your sounds and words flow on your breath to others.

As you voice these questions, you will feel all sorts of revealing information travel through your body, breath, and voice. Some questions might push you into Third Circle or encourage you to shrink into First. Try to stay in Second Circle throughout. By the end you will have more than just knowledge.

> It is the province of knowledge to speak and it is the privilege of wisdom to listen.   —OLIVER WENDELL HOLMES

> The truth which makes men free is for the most part the truth which men prefer not to hear.   —HERBERT AGAR

As you read my responses to these questions, you might want to contrast them with your own.

Remember to keep breathing.
1. When city dwellers live with a constant, often intrusive soundscape, it dulls their hearing. But this can also be comforting and keep you occupied, distracting you from hearing the things you don't want to hear.

   It is easier to half-listen to your partner's complaints if the TV is on. Our ear desensitizes quickly; within a few days of living beside a motorway or subway station, you stop consciously hearing it. The rush of urban life persuades you that you don't have time to listen.

   Many of the world's population haven't ever experienced the sounds of nature and live in noise with muffled listening abilities. If that is the case, it is harder for them

to connect into Second Circle listening. My rural students
are always better listeners. The silence and stillness in the
countryside can send urban dwellers into panic attacks.
But in fact, if you can stay in Second with nature, you
discover it isn't silent or still but full of sound and movement that you can only hear if you are in Second.

2. Who did you last listen to? Was it a superior or someone
who had something you wanted—good reasons to be in
Second Circle, but extra marks if it was listening without
agenda—a perceived inferior, say, or listening just out of
curiosity.

3. Are the people who listen to you below you at work? Do
they have to listen? If not, doesn't it make you feel great
and special when someone's attention is just on you?
Remember, that's how you make people feel when you listen to them in Second Circle—great and special!

4 & 5. Why don't they or you listen? Are they in First or
Third? Are you both out of Second Circle with each other?
And do you care? If you do care, then you must fight to
stay in Second Circle with them.

6. Without doubt, if the news contained information about
people, places, or topics that you were personally connected to, you would remember it, even if the newscaster
wasn't in Second Circle. If you listened to world events in
Second Circle, you would want to make the world a better
place.

7. If you can't remember discussions with your partner the
next day, then you, your partner, or both of you are not
listening in Second Circle to each other. If that goes on,
the relationship is in trouble and both of you will start to
feel lonely and in despair.

8. If you can't remember what is being discussed at work,
you are either taking your position for granted or already
losing opportunities for promotion. People know, even in
a meeting of twenty employees, whether you are listening in Second Circle. You can be certain the ambitious

are aware and the hugely successful operate with Second
Circle listening.

9 & 10. If music doesn't move you or stay with you, you
aren't listening to it in Second Circle.

11. Missing information means you are not listening in
Second Circle. What about that snide, off-the-cuff comment half-heard by you?

12 & 13. Interruption is a Third Circle trait; switching off
because you assume you already know what's coming is
closer to First Circle. Don't do either because it means you
have missed and will miss important information and are
dismissing people. None of us enjoys being dismissed and
you may alienate others.

14. Do you panic when you hear instructions (First) or
believe you can understand so you don't have to listen
fully (Third)? Or do you expect to fail or are bored at the
prospect of doing the task? Both First Circle. Are you
above the task and really expect someone else to do it?
Third Circle. Listen in Second Circle and you'll get over it.

15 & 16. If these experiences rarely happen to you, then
either you're missing what's going on around you or
no one in your regular company is speaking to you
in Second Circle and you are in danger of fading out
through lack of understanding or stimulation. You might
have to seek out social contacts in stiller, quieter venues.
You may have noticed that intense Second Circle connections happen in the silence of a library or a walk in
the park.

17. One of the greatest seduction techniques in history is to
listen to your beloved. My advice is never be seduced
by someone who doesn't listen to you in Second Circle—
however gorgeous—that is, if you want a relationship as
opposed to just sex.

18. This last question is the most poignant. Children respond
to Second Circle listening from adults and remember it
forever with love. Remember how it made you feel: clear,

loved, and known? That's what you do for others when you listen to them in Second Circle. If there wasn't an attentive adult in your life, then it's harder and more painful for you and the world, but in a way you owe it to yourself to connect to others and experience the unconditional feeling of Second Circle listening.

In the attitude of silence the soul finds the path in a clearer light, and what is elusive and deceptive resolves itself into crystal clearness. Our life is a long and arduous quest after Truth.
　　　　　　　　　　　　　　　　　　　—MAHATMA GANDHI

You hear in the womb, and hearing is the last sense to fade as you die.

Working on Second Circle Listening

- Stay in Second Circle body and breath. Keep the jaw released, breathing calmly and deeply throughout.
- Seek out silence. You won't ever find complete silence, but by seeking it, you will engage and work your Second Circle listening. If you accept background noise and become dimmed by it you will not leave First or Third Circle, because sound is not involving you fully.
- Sit and listen to nature, even if it is just in your local park. Stay still and listen with your eyes shut. Peel away sounds. Acknowledge the closest sound and listen through it to the next one. See how far you can hear.
- Now move in the other direction. Identify the closest sound to you and then start listening to your body. Listen to the sound your clothes make, your breath, your swallowing, your heart, and the blood in your veins.
- Turn off the TV, the radio, and any music. Sit in your room and peel the sounds away.
- Repeat both journeys that you performed in nature.

- How many sounds can you hear?
- Listen to your favorite piece of music. Sit still, eyes shut.
- Gradually turn the volume down but still listen intently to the music.
- How low can the volume get before you lose interest because you can't hear properly?
- Listen to your favorite song and really aim to hear the words.
- If you normally go to concerts with amplified music, try to hear music naturally. Seek out concerts of early music played on the original instruments—you will notice how acute your hearing has to become.
- On a journey, count the number of different sounds you can hear.
- In a noisy environment, fix your ear on one sound in the space and aim to hear through all the sounds around you until you tune in to the chosen sound.
- Even for limited amounts of time, listen in Second Circle to people you habitually interrupt or find boring. They might inform you and you might learn something from them. You will definitely change them, and your relationship with them, for the better.
- Listen to the people who serve you and you will get better service because they are rarely noticed, let alone heard.
- Try to identify and name voices passing your office and your home.
- Listen to the news knowing that you should be able to list each item an hour later. Record the news and see how well you've done.
- Listen to your child and partner consciously in Second Circle in the morning and when you and/or they return in the evening.

Practice any of these exercises three times a day and you will gain greater contact with the world around you. You will also find that you are noticed more positively. Any breakdown of communication around you will show some signs of healing. You will hear things you don't want to hear, but at least you will face the truth accurately.

Here are one poet's words upon hearing a skylark singing:

> . . . Teach me half the gladness
>   That thy brain must know;
> Such harmonious madness
>   From my lips would flow,
> The world should listen then—as I am listening now.
>   —PERCY BYSSHE SHELLEY, *"To a Skylark"*

12

Senses

The insights provided in the chapter on listening can be applied to your other senses, particularly sight. You could substitute the words "looking" for "listening," and "seeing" for "hearing," and improve your sight as well as your hearing.

Sight

Already you know that eye contact is a fundamental in Second Circle, and in many communication manuals it is encouraged as a great power tool. It is so, but only if it is done in Second Circle.

Already you can make or recognize the rather dead-eye, detached contact of First or the too judgmental, non-specific Third Circle eye contact.

If your body is in Second Circle and is filled with Second Circle breath, then your eyes will follow. Alternatively, if your eyes become engaged in Second Circle, then your body and breath will follow.

A Second Circle gaze is extremely powerful for you and the object of the gaze; so much so that you know when you are being looked at, even from behind, when you are in Second

Circle. Anyone speaking in public using Second Circle eye contact will be more likely to keep the attention of their audience. This applies to other senses as well.

Taste

Eat a meal in Second Circle. You will taste the food differently. Suddenly junk will taste like junk, good food will taste good.

Notice that eating while watching TV makes the food suffer. Prepare a meal in Second.

Try having a meal with someone at which you both stay in Second with each other and the food. A family eating together in Second Circle creates a good union. Third Circle eating can appear greedy or rushed. At its height, you are not even tasting it. First Circle eating ignores the food and takes it for granted. Both options reduce the satisfaction you desire from food.

I haven't tested this theory as I'm not qualified, but I strongly suspect that Second Circle eating would help weight control and probably also help with drinking problems. You know you're going to get drunk when you start knocking back alcohol in Third Circle, or that you have a drinking problem when you hide your drinking, even from yourself, by drinking in First.

In Third or First drinking, you can drink bad wine or spirits without registering that its quality could strip the paint off a fireplace. Good wine, coffee, and tea drunk in Second are a great joy. Staying in Second as you drink, which takes extra attention if you are getting intoxicated, helps you realize when you've had enough and it's time to stop. If your partner or someone you know well is an addict, you know and dread the moment they click out of Second and get lost to their addiction in either First or Third.

Smell

Try smelling flowers, perfume, food, coffee, and the air in Second Circle. You will immediately awaken the scent in you, hence the saying, "Wake up and smell the coffee."

Equally, notice how a bad smell closes you down into First or turns your nose up into Third.

Touch

The most obvious example of touch is the handshake: the over-strong Third Circle one, the limp First Circle one, and the balanced, uncluttered Second Circle one.

Extend this further, into kissing. You remember Third and First Circle kissing with horror, but the Second Circle kiss, if desired, is gorgeous. Sex in Second Circle is lovemaking.

Touch is so intimate in Second Circle that when it carries the wrong message and is unwanted, it can be at the center of court cases.

People who have to touch as part of their profession—doctors, nurses, dentists, masseurs—need to be able to touch in Second Circle without sexual agenda. If they can't, they resort to Third or First, which always feels dehumanizing.

Try stroking a dog in First and you'll hardly be noticed. In Third it's likely the dog won't enjoy the stroke; but in Second you'll get a good response.

13

Mind

"Curiouser and curiouser!" cried Alice.
—LEWIS CARROLL, *Alice's Adventures in Wonderland*

The Mind in Second Circle

Curiosity only becomes meaningful in Second Circle. Similarly, the passionate expression of what you believe is the truth is only tangible to you and the world when expressed in Second Circle. When passion is expressed in First Circle, it is bottled up and chokes you; and if expressed in Third Circle, it will appear to be prejudiced and unavailable to change and debate.

A man should never be ashamed to own he has been in the wrong, which is but saying, in other words, that he is wiser today than he was yesterday. —ALEXANDER POPE

The human mind is naturally curious; our survival as a species depends on curiosity. To be curious, our attention has to be in Second Circle. Occasionally you might withdraw into First Circle to reflect on a discovery, but you search and find truth and knowledge in Second. Deep knowledge and understanding are only possible in Second Circle, as is their communication to others. You can pass exams by cramming or speed reading (both activities are done in Third Circle), but that knowledge is never remembered a few years later or understood in a profound and human way. Einstein said, "It is a miracle that curiosity survives formal education."

Curiosity and knowledge manifest themselves fully in Second Circle. We come naturally into Second Circle energy when feeling passionate about what we are thinking, saying, and expressing.

If you are honest about what you think and feel, you are in Second Circle with yourself, even if you lie to the world about your thoughts and feelings. Honesty requires presence and truth, and when shared, means you stand by your words. Freedom of speech becomes tension of speech when we are unable to be present with ideas and express them in Second Circle.

Here's a question to wrestle with: Why, if curiosity is so essential to human development and survival, do we so often close down away from Second Circle when we encounter new or different ideas?

This is, of course, the curse of intolerance. We can choose to stay in Second Circle even if we do not approve of an idea, instead of shutting the mind away from an unpleasant thought. You don't have to withdraw into First or oppose the idea by shouting it down in Third. Nothing has ever changed in our history by either being ignored or forced away.

> In every cry of every man,
> In every Infant's cry of fear,
> In every voice, in every ban,
> The mind-forg'd manacles I hear.
> —WILLIAM BLAKE, "London"

The shift away from Second Circle when meeting a new concept curbs curiosity and chains minds. This movement of energy comes from those who lead us. Our leaders or heads—which is an appropriate title in a chapter on Mind—are in a position to either free or block ideas. The heads of countries, corporations, schools, and families actually control whether those in their care can think creatively and passionately. Good, productive leaders operate in Second Circle, and they are present, listening and connected to new ideas. They might not agree with an idea you express and they might have to put boundaries around your actions or even stop you; but because they hear the idea and stay present with it, the boundaries are understood.

It is an act of survival to stay open to an idea you don't want to hear, even if you passionately oppose it. At least listening to it in Second and trying to understand it gives important insights that if ignored (First) or not fully comprehended (Third) could lead to real destruction. Part of curiosity is to know your enemies and what they are thinking.

Uncreative leaders operate in Third Circle. They control and force their ideas, without even properly acknowledging other points of view. They generally bully their way to power and try to make us all see their views as the only ones that exist.

Very occasionally, you can meet a First Circle leader: they normally have enjoyed money and power since infancy and take the whole leadership issue as a given. It has never occurred to them that their way is to be questioned. If they stay in First Circle and take their power for granted, they may well have it usurped by a younger family member or an employee. Shakespeare's Richard II is an example of a First Circle leader who has never had to understand power. This king was crowned when a boy, and was surrounded by yes-men and flatterers who allowed him to misuse his power. It is easy to manipulate leaders who are not in Second Circle as they are prone to flattery.

You know it is perfectly safe and even pleasurable to discuss ideas in Second Circle with your leader if they share your opinions. The test is whether you and your leader can stay connected to each other in Second when your ideas clash; and if you can't, who goes where in terms of energy.

14

The Truth Behind the Clichés

"Standing By What You Say"

Many expressions that have become clichés are nonetheless accurate in their truth. "To stand by what you say," when reexamined, is accurate because if you speak an idea that you are passionate about and believe to be true, then you do have to stand, breathe, and voice it with full Second Circle presence. Only then will it impact on the world; and after speaking this truth, you will have to stand and take the full consequences of your utterance.

If you speak a truth in First Circle body, breath, and voice, you are shrinking from it and apologizing for it. Hearing it spoken in First, listeners don't notice its full importance.

Speak a truth in Third Circle body, and you are hammering it home as though you don't trust the truth. Hearing it spoken in Third, listeners are turned off by the idea and won't bother to assess it with curiosity.

Knowing What You Believe

Here is an exercise for you:

- Write out as succinctly as possible ten ideas that you believe to be true. This might be easy for you, but if you're struggling, I find that dwelling on the idea of justice and what is fair will get the ideas flowing. We all have clear memories of injustices perpetrated on ourselves or on others—that should help you consolidate a list.
- With your list in hand, center your body. Release any tensions in your knees, spine, shoulders, and jaw. Breathe calmly, as low into the body as you can. You might need to walk around or push against a wall to feel Second Circle energy in your body and breath.
- Find a point across the room and breathe to it. Touch the point with Second Circle breath. Hum to the point so you send your voice out in Second Circle.
- Read your list without voice but still with Second Circle energy. Keep physically centered. Keep breathing low.
- Observe what happens to your body and breath.
- As the ideas and your truth pass through you in this open and connected stance, you might want to do all or some of the following:

  Pull back onto your heels

  Tuck your head in

  Look down into the floor

  Collapse your spine and chest

  Your breathing might get shallow or even stop.

These are First Circle reactions in your body. You are apologizing for what you believe. Conversely, a Third Circle bludgeoning of the truth will manifest in these reactions:

A lifting up of your chest, pulling back your head

Your stance might widen, your focus generalize, and your
energy penetrate beyond the room

Your breath might be pulled in with force

- Fight these energy shifts in your body and breath. Keep
  reading the list until you feel you can physically stay and
  breathe in Second Circle.
- Next, vocalize your list. Send it out to the point of focus,
  without devoicing or pushing the words out to the point
  of focus. Don't fall off the words or be too emphatic with
  them. Just say them with clear, uncluttered energy. Release
  the ideas into the world without force or apology.

Even speaking one idea and sending it out of you in Second
is a huge achievement. You will feel open yet decisive. You
mean what you say.

Knowing What You Don't Believe

- Now write a list of ten ideas that you passionately disagree
  with.
- Repeat the work.

As you begin to speak out this list, anger might bubble up. If
it does, then note how you want to deal with the anger. Explode
it out in Third Circle or implode into First Circle. Throughout,
work to keep your body, breath, and voice in Second Circle.
Avoid crossing your arms, fidgeting, and shuffling.

- Following the same processes of Second Circle work, read
  aloud some views you don't hold. This could include political or spiritual beliefs and excerpts from newspapers, be
  they reports or editorials.

Remember, you don't have to approve of what you say, but try to stay in Second Circle. Be very diligent and don't allow cynicism (First), mocking, or ridicule (Third) into your voice. You should communicate the ideas without comment.

- Choose an idea and imagine you are a highly paid lawyer who has to defend it. List seven points to defend this idea and speak those points in Second Circle.

Entering Another World: "Walk a Mile in My Shoes"

In the case of dissension, never dare to judge until you've heard the other side.   —EURIPIDES

You have worked on your own belief systems, but you should also try to move toward other worlds. This next task will take more time but can be fascinating to work on.

- Fix your mind on a real character, dead or alive, either known personally to you or through reputation. Choose someone whose views or lifestyle you *don't* agree with.
- Research the character. Is this person male or female? Rich or poor? Educated or uneducated? Trapped or free? What have you learned about the person's upbringing and environment? Did this person have choice or no choices?
- Try to find sympathy with them. Then return to the ideas they held or deeds they committed and speak them in Second Circle, aloud and freely.

Have you experienced any change of attitude or even empathy? Perhaps not, but what you will find in yourself is a greater openness to them; you will feel less closed off, and therefore more able to deal rationally with their views and belief system. You are safer knowing and understanding their views than not.

When you meet people openly and listen to their views, their lives enrich you and give your own life greater depth.

Great people meet change in Second Circle. Of course, they might reject parts of a person, but by remaining in Second with them, there is always a chance of learning, even from an enemy, and eventually this will make both parties grow.

Winston Churchill could confront and attack a fellow politician across the House of Commons, but two hours later he would be sitting with that person and discussing horse racing. He was able to accept differences but still appreciate shared interests.

I was very moved and engaged by a recent documentary. Simply filmed, it told the story of a middle-class suburban housewife with clear right-wing ideas, who started a correspondence with an inmate on death row. Her letters were initially formal and in Third Circle, but gradually the two corresponded in Second Circle and she found in herself the capacity to love unconditionally a man she had at first patronized and judged. She communicated with him by telephone, the only time they spoke, just before his execution. This woman's world will never be the same again, and casual, untested judgements on any other human being are now impossible for her.

The plays of George Bernard Shaw are master classes in open debate. Characters with opposing views are placed in an arena and you watch them struggle with each other's views. If played properly, the audience is swung from one view to another without prejudice, and although you make up your own mind, you learn by hearing different perspectives voiced by articulate people. The characters listen to each other and change if and when they accept a new idea. No one is stuck in an entrenched position. Shaw has a lot to teach us about our minds in Second Circle.

> Don't criticize what you don't understand, son. You never walked in that man's shoes.   —ELVIS PRESLEY

15

Heart

Wheresoever you go, go with all your heart.
—Confucius

We can block our hearts as effectively as we can block our minds. Guilt, shame, and fear can rapidly shift you out of your presence into First or Third Circle. This shift is an initial and natural reaction in order to bury, deny, or ridicule the emotion.

We all sometimes disapprove of our feelings and those of others. But this disapproval doesn't help us to survive and be enlightened. Survival is only possible in Second Circle, as is knowledge. It is better to own your true feelings and shadows, and to know what others feel about you. Believe me, you are putting yourself and others at risk if you don't care for your heart with presence. As Sarah in Arnold Wesker's *Chicken Soup with Barley* puts it, "You've got to care, you've got to care or you'll die."

Three Stories

The three stories below changed my heart and helped me to grow up emotionally. They all affected my heart.

The first is about the power of hatred.

I was teaching in India. One day, after giving a master class in an Indian university outside Madras, I was ushered into the Principal's office for tea. His greeting was formal and the ceremony of serving the perfect English tea was impeccable. I was overanimated, as I had enjoyed the class and was rather pleased with myself and in Third Circle. He was polite but withdrawn. Definitely First Circle.

After some minutes he went quiet, looked into his teacup, and stirred it. I felt a change of energy and we both shifted into Second Circle. He looked up at me and I experienced the power of his eyes suddenly penetrating me. "I hate the British and what your Empire did to my country." For a moment I thought my heart would stop and never start again.

I had never experienced such savage hatred—in a way, the civilized surroundings made the hate worse, but I managed to stay facing him in Second. In that moment I had to actually face the wrongs of my country and the lies I had been taught at school. I knew those wrongs and lies intellectually and politically, but not emotionally. Even worse, I had to face my own emotional stupidity and insensitivity.

I stayed in Second with him. I heard a clock tick. We were now breathing together—it was gladiatorial, and the energy was getting darker with each tick. In the mid-eighties the United States and Europe were facing the AIDS crisis. He smiled at me. "I'm glad you have the plague of AIDS. The sins of the father will be visited on the sons." At that I got up and left the room, devastated and shocked, but enlightened and hopefully a more sensitive and prepared guest.

I learned that political awakening comes through the heart and is personal. Not only did he hate my nation but he hated me, both with good reason. And to my only credit, I took the meeting as a revelation in Second Circle.

The second story is about hatred and survival of a different kind:

I lived with a man but the relationship was doomed as he was an alcoholic and, like all drinkers, abusive. I believed that love would change him. But he was in Second Circle with the gin and tonic, and not with me. He couldn't feel my love. Over the years, I withdrew into First Circle in an attempt to survive and stay. Although I knew intellectually that it was not safe, my heart was so deadened that I couldn't move, and even though I was teaching actors to breathe, I was hardly oxygenated myself.

One morning at 2 a.m., my partner was asleep and dead drunk, or so I thought, and I was sitting alone again, dazed with grief in the living room. Suddenly the door burst open, which shocked me into Second Circle. My partner entered with a knife, sober enough to be in a vivid Second, and shouted at me, "You are a monster and should be destroyed!" I got up, pushed him over, and left, never to return.

We had met in Second and the intimate violence of that meeting shook me into action. I knew that if he didn't actually knife me in that moment, he would find a way, however subtle, to cut out my heart.

Here's a final story about a meeting that changed all my perceptions of beauty and sexual desire:

I was thirty-two and teaching in Eastern Europe. A brilliant and famous director had watched me work and invited me out for dinner. The whole meal was an intense Second Circle exchange. We enthralled each other. My mind, heart, and spirit engaged with his. I should explain that he was eighty-four and, up to that moment, I had no conception that I could find an old man attractive.

Second Circle connections of the heart do not necessarily fit into the neat boxes of conformity. Your true Second Circle emotions can cross unimaginable frontiers. Second Circle encounters of the heart on any level will transform your life. You will never be the same again, which is why, if you are afraid of change when feelings grip you, you might resist staying in Second Circle.

All intimate exchanges are (or should be) in Second Circle—shared energy that gives you knowledge of someone else's world. At that moment, you may fall in love.

"*To fall in love*": what a clear description that is. In order to fall, you have to let go. Let go of what? Your Third Circle defenses or your First Circle self?

When you love someone, that person becomes your constant Second Circle focus. Their presence enters your heart and mind, and if they fall for you, then a great love story begins.

> My true-love hath my heart, and I have his,
> By just exchange one for the other given.
> I hold his dear, and mine he cannot miss:
> There never was a bargain better driven.
> His heart in me keeps me and him in one;
> My heart in him his thoughts and senses guides:
> He loves my heart, for once it was his own;
> I cherish his because in me it bides.
> His heart his wound received from my sight;
> My heart was wounded with his wounded heart;
> For as from me on him his hurt did light,
> So still, methought, in me his hurt did smart:
> Both equal hurt, in this change sought our bliss,
> My true-love hath my heart and I have his.
>   —SIR PHILIP SIDNEY, from *Arcadia*

In order to see and notice someone fully, and therefore love them, you have to be in Second Circle; and for that love to fade and die, you will have either withdrawn from the once beloved into First Circle or defended yourself from them in Third.

If you are to love and cherish someone over time, you have to stay with them in Second Circle and, even harder, allow them to be themselves in Second. This allows for change, aging, fading beauty, and all the tempests that life offers you both equally.

. . . Love is not love
Which alters when it alteration finds . . .
O, no! it is an ever-fixed mark
That looks on tempests and is never shaken . . .
Love's not Time's fool . . .
Love alters not with his brief hours and weeks,
But bears it out even to the edge of doom . . .
—WILLIAM SHAKESPEARE, Sonnet 116

This is Shakespeare's description of Second Circle equal and therefore unconditional love. The lover allows the beloved to alter and transform.

You fall in love in Second Circle but fall out of love if you become a First Circle victim to your love or a Third Circle controller of it. If you love only to service your First Circle self or your Third Circle image, then that love is conditional and will not survive.

Whatever dies was not mixed equally.
—JOHN DONNE, "The Good-Morrow"

Matters of the heart and all the passions that pass through it are infinitely complex: to feel completely all your love, rage, desire, grief, joy, and fear in Second Circle takes courage as you are sometimes bearing the unbearable.

You must go on, I can't go on, I'll go on.
—SAMUEL BECKETT, *The Unnamable*

As you experience all the feelings you didn't want to feel or have not been allowed to feel due to your upbringing or culture, the overwhelming temptation is to withdraw into First or bluff your way out of the feeling in Third Circle. First Circle reduces the heart and Third Circle aims to deny it.

First Circle emotional reduction includes trivializing a passion, assuming a carelessness toward it, or taming it with sentimentality. Third Circle denials can involve mocking the emotions and becoming cynical toward them, either in yourself or when observed in others. When you stay with a feeling in Second Circle, you begin to know what you feel and how that feeling affects you.

> And now good-morrow to our waking souls,
> Which watch not one another out of fear . . .
> JOHN DONNE, "The Good-Morrow"

In Second Circle, you have the chance to be awakened to your passions and watch others without fear. Fear is the mask that disables the passion in your mind and heart. It is a subject that we all know a great deal about, and it is one that I spend most days of my working life minimizing in performers.

A performer consciously looks into the eyes of fear several times a day. Fear inhabits performers' bodies, breath, minds, hearts, creativity, self-esteem—and more. Whenever they feel safe, fear pops up beside them.

> As an unperfect actor on the stage
> Who with his fear is put besides his part . . .
> —WILLIAM SHAKESPEARE, Sonnet 23

Everyone in a rehearsal room knows that everyone else is fearful. This shared knowledge is a luxury that most non-performers rarely experience. Fear is the secret that knee-jerks you out of Second Circle, away from thoughts and feelings you cannot meet. Yet, by not meeting these passions, you narrow your life, disconnecting yourself from greater knowledge and power.

Spirit

As we feel great love, we often experience the presence of our soul, and our spirit feels concrete; it fuses our bodies, minds, and hearts.

The body is a device to calculate the astronomy of the spirit.

—RUMI

There is a famous Hindu story about a man looking for God. He was in a library reading book after book and God said to him, "I am here." The man shouted back, "Shut up. I am looking for God."

Most religions prescribe that in order to experience a divine presence, you have to be present yourself. This is the conclusion that Ronald Eyre came to after his brilliant twenty-six-hour documentary *The Long Search*. Here are his words over visuals of a Buddhist monk doing a walking meditation, bare feet connecting fully to the earth and breath fully felt in the body, both necessary functions to being present:

> This attention to breathing, to being where you are deserves a better name than "mysticism." I'd call it the practice of presence, of being where you are. Present and knowing it. If the fear of death has a solvent and joy at being alive has a pivot—here is where I'm going to have to look for them.

With that presence, you can not only meet the Divine, but encounter the divinity in other humans. You will find balance, humanity, and equality. This meeting is frighteningly absent from the Third Circle fervor of fundamentalism.

Many stories describe how the Buddha found the middle way. I like this one:

> The Buddha was sitting under a tree beside a river in Gaya, his body wasted with deprivation. He was in deep meditation. A boat floated down the river and on the boat was a

guru teaching his pupils how to play the sitar. Through his trance the Buddha heard the guru saying, "If you tune the sitar too tightly, the note will go sharp. If you tune it too loosely, it will go flat. You must tune it just so." The boat drifted by and the Buddha came to and saw a young girl passing with a bowl of rice. He asked for some rice and ate.

The middle way. Not too harsh on yourself, not too indulgent, but just so—centered and balanced, aware of life, humanity, and equality. The Buddha's middle way is one of presence and lives in the Second Circle.

16
Rest

At this point we have worked on your whole presence through the energy of your body, breath, voice, speech, mind, and heart, and we have also briefly touched on spirit. You have indeed started the journey. If you now only interact with people who have your best interests in their body, mind, heart, and spirit, you could stay whole in Second Circle.

Of course this is idealistic, not only because most of the people we meet don't love us unconditionally and some may even want to hurt us, but because there is more to consider. Unfortunately, it is impossible to travel any distance in life without some experience of loss, which can lead to heightened pain. This loss, pain, and despair can make us lose our presence; it can take us out of ourselves and sometimes requires a concerted effort to reconnect to our world.

Some of us have families, friends, and lovers who conspire to destroy our presence and knock us continually out of our Second Circle. Then there are the jobs some people have that make it easy to switch off even when the work really demands Second Circle.

I have called this chapter "Rest," as you should now begin to rest on the knowledge that you have already gained. This will help you to stay positively present before we tackle the people and events in your life that will constantly challenge your well-being and Second Circle energy.

You must trust that you have important reserves and strategies for staying present in your body. You can recenter, reenergize, and refocus your body into Second Circle after any event that pushes you into First Circle body or pulls you up into Third Circle body. You now have breath exercises to keep your breath free and touching the world. Use these exercises when life distorts your vital oxygen supply.

You don't need to stay with an underpowered voice or rely on an overpushed one, as both voices will only alienate you from the world and keep you away from Second Circle communication. If and when you feel your mind, heart, and spirit close down or become overblown and judgmental, you can rest, adjust, and reengage their presence.

Appreciating Beauty

You should be able to practice listening, reading, speaking, thinking, feeling, seeing, and touching in Second Circle, and as a result you will find that you absorb the world more clearly. It would be interesting for you to revisit museums, galleries, landscapes, houses, books, poems, and music that you believe you know, and experience them differently and more deeply in Second Circle.

Perhaps you have started to take the beauty of the world around you for granted. In Second Circle, the original life force of iconic symbols is resurrected in your presence. After all, one of the functions of an artist is to jolt, even shock us into the present; to engage us and reeducate our ability to look, listen, and experience the world around us. Consequently, one of the reasons artists reinvent forms and break rules is to shock our complacency and to help us see, hear, feel, and think anew.

In the early Renaissance, Masaccio painted an ugly Virgin

Mary, which shocked the world. Later, Beethoven broke with classical music forms and enraged his audiences. The Beatles wrote lyrics that really meant something, rendering the lyrical content of song writing as powerful as the musical structure.

The Power of Known Icons

In Second Circle, try some of the following:

- Look again at familiar paintings.
- Look up at sacred buildings or other buildings that you pass regularly, and notice the devoted work in their fabric.
- Listen to music that you thought you knew well and hear it deepen.
- Look at symbols you see everywhere, such as a flag, a crucifix, or a subway map.
- Read words you think you know, like the National Anthem, the Lord's Prayer, the Declaration of Independence; poems and ideas you take for granted.
- Look at some photos and films that have changed the consciousness of the world. For example, the liberation of Buchenwald; the devastation of Hiroshima; the lone boy in Tiananmen Square stopping a tank.

These images seem even more profound in Second Circle. What becomes apparent as you look, listen, and read is whether the work will last. Indeed, you might realize what constitutes good and bad art! Even if you don't like a work in Second Circle, you can appreciate its value. Many successful works don't bear scrutiny in Second Circle as they haven't been forged with present energy.

Lastly, revisit the milestones in your life and education, and experience them again presently, with clarity and new meaning.

17

Working with Your Fear

Fear is an inescapable part of life, but it can be reduced, even rendered harmless. We are going to work on fear in Second Circle. Please be gentle with yourself; if any of this seems too difficult and distressing at any stage, stop. You are working on transforming deep energies and you are not a failure if you find certain changes initially unbearable. You might surprise yourself as the monster could prove to be an illusion. Remember the Wizard of Oz: he seemed to have all that power, but was only a little old man pulling levers.

Facing the Fear

Do this exercise in a safe place where you know you will not be disturbed.

- Lie on the floor on your back, with your legs propped up on a facing chair. The chair should be at the right height to comfortably support your calf muscles, so that your thighs can stay unclamped. Put a thin book or cushion under your head.
- A low, deep breath not only oxygenates you but awakens your emotions. Like your body, emotion has movement and

needs air. During this exercise, keep the breath as low as possible. Exchange the breath as quietly as you can.

• As the exercise progresses, you may cry, and feel your body and breath wanting to pull away from the fear. In Third Circle, this will start in the lifting of the sternum and holding your breath; or in First Circle, your shoulders will sag.

• As you lie on your back, breathe deeply and start to speak your fears in Second Circle: "I am frightened of . . ."

• Start with objects or animals, e.g., spiders, certain foods, snakes, knives, dogs, telephones, tall buildings.

• Move on to events, e.g., a visit to the dentist, speaking in public, entering a roomful of people, standing on a subway platform.

• Now tackle people, e.g., a parent, your boss, your partner, your brother or sister.

• Now name fears of people or events from your past. Are they still there? What do you fear in the present? What do you fear in the future?

You will find that by speaking them out in Second Circle, all these fears begin to lose their potency.

Your emotional reactions to this exercise will help you identify how you deal with fear. First Circle tactics include trying to please, to be liked, or to flee from the fear. Third Circle tactics include aiming to destroy or control the fear.

If this exercise is useful, you can repeat it every few weeks. You will discover that certain fears evaporate; the ones that don't must be addressed as they are stopping you feeling fully in your heart in Second Circle.

Knowing your fears is an important window to knowing yourself. Knowing yourself is the most creative, interesting, and difficult journey you will make, and no one can do that journey for you. You cannot start the journey or sustain it unless you encounter yourself—your heart and mind—and the hearts and minds of others in Second Circle.

"Know thyself"—these words greeted visitors who went to consult the Oracle at Delphi in Greece 2,500 years ago, and the journey continues.

> What a piece of work is a man! How noble in reason! How infinite in faculty! In form and moving, how express and admirable! In action, how like an angel! In apprehension, how like a god! The beauty of the world! The paragon of animals!   —WILLIAM SHAKESPEARE, *Hamlet*

Human beings are indeed amazing. You mustn't let fear block your full potential—but it will do so if ignored.

18

Defending
Your
Presence

Before we move on to face the daily challenges of life, we need to consider some technical strategies to aid you when your Second Circle energy is under threat.

Such circumstances are always complex. However, the more you remain in Second Circle, the more aware you will be of any growing complexities. You will pick up danger signs early in a way that you cannot do when you are in First or Third Circle. In those Circles, it is often the case that the threat and its accompanying danger have doubled, if not trebled, before your internal alarm bell jolts you into survival.

You will need two fundamental strategies:

1. How to stay in Second when one or more people are pulling you into First or Third Circle; and
2. How to guide a First or Third Circle person or group into Second Circle.

These two strategies are positive ones. There are moments in life when you might need a second set of strategies:

1. How to withdraw from Second into First or Third Circle; and
2. How to move into Second from First or Third Circle.

How to Stay in Second Circle

Anyone threatening you will use their own strategies to try to weaken you, to contain you in First Circle, or to force you into an aggressive Third and create more conflict.

It is hard to stay in Second when others are depressing you into First or goading you into Third. But both shifts mean that you have "lost it." You can see this by watching the highly focused Second Circle soccer player who, when insulted by another player, moves foolishly into Third, fouls the other player, and gets sent off the field. Or the shift of energy in a confrontation when needless and thoughtless violence takes place as one or both parties lose their patience and hit out in Third.

If you spend any time with a group of First Circle people, you will find yourself retreating into their energy. We have all entered a room at work or a social gathering and felt the First Circle energy. We then know we are in for a dreadful and depressing time. My advice is: try to gauge this type of energy at job interviews, as it is only changed from the top.

The Circle of energy you meet might encourage your energy to move in the opposite direction. First Circle gatherings might force you into Third, or Third Circle energy might have you retreating into First.

Begin to identify the shifts in your energy when people try to change you and reduce your full Second Circle power. These are the qualities that you should be retaining when other energy is around you or attempting to change you:

Body: Shoulders open, upper chest released, jaw unclenched, centered, head positioned on top of the spine, spine placed, feet on the floor, knees unlocked

Breath: Calm and silent, going deep into the body and opening the ribs and lower abdominal area. You are breathing to points of focus outside yourself, touching where you are focusing

Eyes: Focusing on the world around you

Voice: Free, open, and directed outward to the people you are addressing

Ears: Alert, listening to people

Heart and head: Curious, non-judgmental, full of sense and feeling

The following shifts can be very subtle, but with practice you will begin to recognize them.

Shifts into First can include:

Body: Shoulders rounding, chest and spine depressing, head slumping, body wriggling or fidgeting

Breath: Swallowing or completely holding the breath; panic in the breath

Eyes: Vision blurring—the color dulled

Voice: Weakening and trailing off; giving up

Ears: Finding it harder to listen

Heart and head: Bored, powerless, mind and heart wandering; thinking and worrying about yourself

Shifts into Third can include:

Body: Stiffening and lifting throughout the shoulders, chest, spine, and jaw; a rigid stance

Breath: Noisy and deliberately taken; locked when inflated. Breathing past the people and space you are in. Taking too much breath

Eyes: Glaring and scanning rather than looking

Voice: Too loud, too insistent, forcing energy. Interrupting—drowning others out; pushed

Ears: Picking out the things you want to hear and ignoring others

Heart and head: Feeling you have to force something. Judgmental, often desperately trying to change others'

opinions. Attempting to control the emotional and intellectual climate

The most immediate changes to make if you wish to stay in
Second are:

Adjust the body tensions—shoulders, upper chest, spine, jaw,
knees—and keep a centered stance.

Breathe calmly, silently, and deeply to the person or group.
Keep your voice open; do not speak too fast (Third) or too
slow (First). Sustain the voice without pushing.

Look, listen, feel, and think without objectivity and with
curiosity.

All these adjustments can be done without anyone seeing
them. Although it might be hard to stay in Second, by doing so
you won't feel drained or defeated by meetings and events as
you would be were you to be drawn away from yourself, out of
Second Circle.

How to Guide Others into Second Circle

The most important understanding is that there is no way you
can guide anyone out of First or Third *unless you are in Second
yourself.* You have to evaporate their fear of you by adopting a
caring and non-judgmental Second Circle.

Sometimes, heightening Second throughout your body
and breath will draw (First) or drop (Third) people into their
Second.

If you feel safe with someone, you can help them into Second
by touching their arm and getting clear eye contact with them.
Don't rush this, but wait for the contact to happen.

You can do this eye contact with a group. Looking around
and aiming to achieve eye contact can bring everyone into

Second. In the same way, you can touch people into Second by breathing to them until they respond. It is possible to breathe a whole group into Second.

Keep in Second while you speak. Don't be tempted to raise your voice or be subdued. By displaying acute Second Circle listening, you can draw someone into your energy. As long as you don't sound too critical, but caring and interested, you can ask questions to get a person to reach out to you. In this way, you can regulate people if they are too quiet or too loud.

Showing interest in a First Circle person can draw them into Second. Use simple and direct questions. A Third Circle person often drops into Second when you ask them to explain in more detail something they are talking about. Make them personalize information and feel rather than think. Whatever happens, stay in Second yourself.

How to Withdraw from Second into First or Third Circle

There are occasions when you will need to absent yourself from Second Circle, for example, when a person (or persons) is annoying you, perhaps by being too intrusive. Vacating is a better option than confronting them. You can either retreat (First) or defend yourself by putting a barrier up (Third).

These movements are only appropriate if you don't anticipate danger or have no sense of real malice from those around you. You will have to choose whether you want to appear retiring or defended.

To move into First, you need to slightly collapse through your body and breathe a shallow breath. These physical actions will switch you off. Moving into First will probably seem less offensive to those around you than the option of Third Circle, but you will be less defended. To become a fully defended Third, draw yourself up through your shoulders and chest, lift up and tighten your spine, take a few large breaths, and you will be in a defended Third.

If there is danger, you will have to learn to mix Circles. You could appear physically in First or Third but in actuality stay alert in a hidden and intense Second. You will be following the physical instructions of either First or Third but will still be listening, thinking, and feeling in Second.

The choice between showing First or Third is dictated by understanding the nature of danger. First will make you appear casual and cool, maybe more of a victim. Third will be more of a challenge to others around and could provoke attention, but it could also subdue.

You will have felt this mixture of Circles if you are on a bus or train that is suddenly occupied by out-of-order kids. You stay connected to them but feign a First Circle interest in a book or look out of the window.

How to Move into Second from Third or First Circle

These maneuvers are essential when you realize that a person or a situation requires your full attention. Perhaps you have misjudged someone's needs or the gravitas of a moment, or you may be shocked by an event and need to move quickly into survival mode.

If you are in First, lift up through your spine, release your shoulders, breathe to the person or room, and make clear eye and ear contact. If you are in Third, release your upper chest (placing a hand there helps), unclench your jaw, calm your breath, and place it back into the space and the people in that space. Listen and look carefully at the person or people concerned. Notice what they are saying and wearing. Don't take anything for granted. Try to think what they are thinking and feel what they are feeling.

Mixing Circles

By now you have realized that the Circle combinations between people are infinite and forever transforming and shifting. You have realized the potential of mixing Circles.

Driving a car and listening to music should be a mix of Second Circle on the road with the music in First. The reason that driving and speaking on a cell phone is potentially lethal is that our attention to the road is pulled from Second Circle into First Circle and our attention to the phone is pulled into Second Circle.

Listening to music on an iPod means you are focused on the music in Second but are vulnerable if you are in unsafe environments. You are in First to the world. Within some peer groups or cliques at work you can observe the group pretending to be disconnected (First) to a teacher or presenter, but individuals within the group who are frightened of being labeled uncool listen in Second. Those are generally people with ambition who are not yet strong enough to show the group their interest. It can work the other way. Imagine the bravado of a gang in Third with one individual more tuned to the world and others in it—in Second. In this instance, the person in Second has more humanity than the rest of the group. That is the person you appeal to if the group turns on you.

You will begin to recognize the mixing of Circles in various people and situations:

- There are those who listen in First and reply to you in Third. They hear what you say through themselves and their experience, not yours, and reply generally.
- Some people listen in Second but reply in First or Third. They have listened to you specifically but choose to reply in a way that bypasses your specificity.
- There are those who detach as you are speaking to them (First) or block you (Third).

- There are those who use Second Circle intimate language but are actually dealing with you in First or Third.
- Think of the sometimes salacious occasions when seemingly Third Circle formal and distancing language is delivered in an inappropriate Second Circle style. For instance, you might know that something insulting or suggestive is being communicated but have no real evidence for that in the language.

Daily Exercises

Chart your way through a day observing the mixing of Circles. Prime events might include:

- Travel—you in First Circle with the surroundings, but in Second Circle with music or a newspaper
- Being bored (First), but having to give the impression that you are doing your job or are interested in what a colleague is saying
- Confronting someone who frightens you—this will be a mix of either Third with Second on alert or First with Second engaged
- Socializing in a noisy bar where only Third Circle communication works, but you must appear to be in Second
- A point when you are distracted by a physical task that seems to have your full Second Circle attention but in actuality you are listening to a conversation in Second and completing the task in First or Third

You should be starting to realize just how skilled you are at moving energies through and around yourself. These daily recognitions of energy in turn will give you more power, understanding, and control over interactions.

19

The
Spoilers

Do unto others as you would
have done unto you.

—THE GOLDEN RULE

When actors lose their presence, they talk about an outside eye
looking at them and judging them. This outside eye is sometimes called "the little fucker" as it spoils the work.

Sadly, in real life there are people out there determined to
spoil your day and erode, if not fully take, your presence. Some
of these "spoilers" are obvious—you know who is likely to spoil
a party if you invite them. Others are more subtle; but I am willing to wager that if you feel your Second Circle energy is under
threat, then you are probably in the presence or have the memory of a spoiler. Indeed, it was a spoiler or spoilers who took
your presence in the first place.

The discussion that follows will explore the effects of spoilers, but it is important to remind ourselves that the two-way
street of intimate Second Circle energy also requires us to be
constantly aware of our own ability to spoil those we interact
with. As soon as we connect to others we have power through
their bodies, minds, hearts, and spirits.

Physical, Sexual, Emotional, Intellectual,
and Spiritual Spoilers

When a spoiler stalks you, threatens you, or abuses you in any
context, they become a predator and you appear to them as a

target. This is because you seem a victim in First Circle. I was once working with a famous ballerina who told me that Rudolf Nureyev dropped her deliberately on her first big break in the Royal Ballet. She had replaced an injured prima ballerina and to her horror, on stage in front of royalty, he dropped her. Years later, she found enough courage to ask him why he had done it. His reply was honest and simple: "Because you let me."

Sometimes a spoiler goes after a Third Circle energy. On these occasions, the victim appears too cocky, pushy, or arrogant. Whole groups can combine to knock you down. In Australia, it is called the "tall poppy syndrome." Anyone who shows their petals above the rest should be chopped down.

Sadly, some Third Circle women meet this force in the guise of sexual harassment. The defense for this spoiling of women is, "it served them right." In the seventies a celebrated British judge told the world that any woman who was raped was "asking for it."

Before working on practical solutions for these threats to your energy, you must consider the following points:

> The containable predators, the ones you can deal with, particularly physically, are Third Circle bullies. They wouldn't take on anyone physically stronger than themselves.
> However, if a bully is in Second Circle, they are very dangerous and you must seek help immediately.

> You must take responsibility for your own energy; that could mean that you have to change that energy drastically around any threat.

> No one can tell you how to survive a threatening encounter as survival is in the moment, and the moment can't be described before the event.

These are only guidelines. The best defense is being in Second Circle all the time when any danger is present.

20

Threats

Physical Threats

Spoilers are people whom you generally know, people you normally encounter regularly. But there are also threats that manifest themselves, as it were, out of the blue. It is essential to be alert and in Second Circle when an environment feels—and is known to be—hostile.

Dark streets, parks, parking lots, rough areas of a city, a forest, an unfamiliar city, the arrival of loud drunks or a group of youths on the lookout for trouble in your space, all create feelings of unease. In any of these environments or scenarios, you would be very unwise not to be in Second Circle or to be doing anything that impedes it. That could include speaking on a cell phone or listening to music on an iPod. It is equally a very bad idea to negotiate a hostile journey home at night across a park or in a cab if you are drunk or have taken drugs. Your Second Circle is impaired and you have become a predator's dream prey.

In certain scenarios, however, such as if you are trapped in a confined space with a threatening force—a bus, a train, a cab—it might be wise to pretend to be in First, reading a book, listening to music, while actively staying very strongly in Second Circle.

You might even adopt a First Circle body image, reducing your presence physically. Moving into Third Circle could encourage an attack but might be effective if the predators are bluffing.

In enclosed environments, check where the nearest exit is and don't wait a second longer than you need to use it. Get off the train, although obviously not on a deserted platform, or change cars, but act sooner rather than later. Our instincts are heightened in Second Circle and we only hesitate in First or Third Circle. So-called "city kids" know how to stay in Second Circle. Both of the other Circles can delude you into thinking the danger is not real or happening. In Second your survival instincts are rarely wrong. Sometimes you will actually feel yourself snap into Second and fully appreciate a danger.

Many of us have been brought up to believe we will be looked after by authorities, police, and so on, but in critical moments of crisis you have only yourself and your presence as a tool for survival. People who have no trust in authorities will act sooner when threatened. If the situation accelerates, and ignoring the predator or mob isn't going to work, you will have to stay in Second and make eye contact.

Remember there are no reliable forms to survival, but here are some suggestions.

Strategies When Threatened

- Avoid Third. Your aggression will only fuel the aggressor's.
- Breathe as low as you can toward the aggressor.
- Stand or sit up in your center.
- Talk to the person calmly, even kindly. This can humanize them and make it more difficult for them to hurt you.
- In a group, try to make eye contact with the leader. The rest will be waiting for their leader's command. This is difficult if they are all drunk, but you might be able to find the most sober member of the gang.

- If there is any opportunity to run, take it.
- If you feel that screaming or shouting would help, do it in Second.

Physical Threats in the Home

In a strange way, environments that encourage us to feel safe can be more dangerous. You relax out of Second Circle into First. This can happen after a long, hard day's work, when you are walking to the car or entering your home. Try to do these things in Second Circle. Don't switch off until you are safely in your car or home and sure that you are really alone, with the door locked.

Any unusual noise in your house should place you in Second Circle immediately. Any stranger entering your home should put you in Second Circle—even if it is a handyman or a mailman you vaguely know. Home should be safe, so threats in your home are intolerable, which is why domestic violence is so vile—anyone abusing you here is spoiling a sacred place of trust and peace. Get them out or get yourself out.

Physical Threats at Work

You should feel safe at work. You cannot work efficiently if you don't. Good workers are in Second Circle, which is impossible if you are being bullied by a colleague or a group of colleagues. Threats and abuse are a form of torture, and it is beyond depressing to have to spend your workday in that kind of atmosphere.

A Checklist for Work

Here are some facts you must assess if you are under threat:

- Are you in First or Third at work? If First, then you are perceived as a victim and easy prey. If Third, then you are annoying to the bully and they want to bring you down.

- Is the bully in Third or Second as they attack? Mostly they are in Third, but if they are in Second they are extremely cruel and dangerous.

- If it is a group, are they in Third in their hostile collusions against you? Or, more cruelly, are they in Second?

You must try to stay in Second with bullies. Stay in your Second Circle body and breath, breathe to them, maintain an open, calm voice and good eye contact. As they enter a room, switch into Second Circle, even if they haven't noticed you.

If you are dealing with Third Circle bullies, your connection to presence and power will throw them off. It will confuse them as you are not behaving as they expect and this might be enough for them to leave you alone and seek another victim. After all, bullies need victims. If you are dealing with a Second Circle bully, such tactics might not work. However, a Second Circle response can lead the bully to turn to their former victim as an ally, even as a friend! I remember standing up to a bully at school when I was nine. She then spent the next seven years trying to be my friend.

In the presence of a bully there are two instinctive reactions. One is to disappear into First. This only works if the bully fixes his or her attention onto someone else. They might not notice you but will abuse another person in the workplace. In First Circle, you are complicit with the bullying and are only waiting for the bully to turn their attention on you, at a later date. And turn they will. The second reaction is to face the bully in Third Circle. This can work if you have equal power and support within the group, but can lead to heightening the conflict, perhaps even to the point of violence. Facing down the bully will get you noticed, but only do this if you can handle the fallout.

How to Face Down an Assailant

- The safest solution when bullied is to maintain a constant Second Circle. Stay physically in Second, breathing to the bully in Second.
- Be extra careful as the bully or bullies enter your space or you theirs. Be careful as you turn your back on them in the space.
- Don't show them First, and stay in Second, through focus and breath, when they are picking on someone else.
- Show sympathy to the victim. Don't ignore the abuse, either toward yourself or others, as it must be witnessed.

It is important that you enter every new situation, job, meeting, party, and so on in Second to clearly signal you are not a victim before you ever relax into First. When nervous or keen to impress, it is easy to enter new situations in Third Circle, but this can make people want to take you down a peg or two. Assess every new situation in Second Circle, listening before you act.

You can observe in any situation the mistakes of a newcomer who wishes to impress too quickly. In their Third Circle keenness, they don't assess situations clearly and jump into trouble by contributing in an overeager way without understanding the power structures in the room. These interlopers will be treated with disdain and receive possible retribution from the group's seasoned participants. Staying in Second gives you a chance accurately to assess each scenario as it arises; to appear strong, sensitive, clear, and caring; and to be noticed in a positive way.

If these strategies don't work, you have some hard choices to make as a bully isn't going to get better, whether you are in First, Second, or Third. Start making notes, documenting the abuse, and begin to assess whether you should leave or go to the bully's boss. You should check the processes the company has in place for dealing with threats. Don't let it spoil and destroy you, because that is what the bully wants.

Are You the Bully?

By this point in the book, you will know whether you yourself have a tendency to bully. We all have, particularly if we have been bullied ourselves, as we have more of an insight into who can be bullied easily.

- If you are a Third Circle bully, you can deal with your tendency by retreating into Second in the victim's presence. If you still have a desire to hurt, retreat further into First.
- Find out something you like or respect about the person. See the world from their point of view.
- If all else fails, avoid their company. Walk away.

Sexual Threats

Certain environments encourage those who may try to harass you sexually. Such places include loud bars, parties, and crowds. The presence of alcohol throws most of us into Third Circle, away from clear sensitivity to others, and weakens our ability to read sexual signs clearly. This drought of Second Circle energy becomes clear when you find that wonderful oasis of Second Circle contact in those overenergized and generalized Third Circle gatherings. If you are in First, you will find it hard to get across a no to a highly charged Third Circle sexual predator; and if you are in Third, you will miss some of the early warning signs.

If you can't stay in Second Circle in a noisy bar, then move quickly into it at the first sign of a threat.

How to Pick Up on Sexual Threats

- If you flirt with someone in Third Circle and you see them shift into Second with you, this is a sure sign that they believe you are willing.
- If you flirt with someone and you are both in Second Circle, then perhaps you have to take responsibility, as it will seem you are willing.
- If you are flirting with someone and they move into First, then they don't want you. Leave them alone as they are probably only tolerating you because you have some power over them.
- If you don't want someone sexually and they are coming on to you, go into Second and tell them so, directly and kindly. Do this as soon as you can. If they continue, then the harassment is clear and intended.

When you are out and about socializing, to some extent you are aware that sexual energy will be present. The harder environments in which to negotiate these threats are the places we don't necessarily expect to be treated as sexual objects: at work, in education, and in the home.

Sexual Threats at Work

At work, particularly if we are bored, sexual flirtations are exciting but very destructive to the workplace. However, this type of activity does not always qualify as full-scale sexual harassment.

Harassment starts when the misuse of power is harnessed to sex. This debate is constantly under scrutiny since women have started to gain power in the workplace. Women have to take responsibility if they misuse their sexual power to gain promotion. Not only does this not work but it taints other women. The "power flirts," as I call them, make it almost impossible for other women to have a business meeting in a bar. I don't really blame women, as many of us have been taught from a very early age to please men. These pleasing techniques are very confusing to men, who may be encouraged to think we find them sexually attractive. Such confusion becomes critical in the workplace when women are striving for power and equality. Women should become more aware of their sexual power through Second Circle; then they can choose not to use it and take responsibility when they do.

All men should try to understand through Second Circle connection to women that these pleasing techniques used by women are formed as a result of society's long-held belief that men hold power over women. Some women appease men because of this long history of masculine power.

The enlightened man must resist the temptation to reduce women's power by sexually harassing them. Equally, enlightened women who wish to avoid sexual harassment mustn't flirt and then complain of harassment, or harass men over whom they have power. A lot of the initial mistakes that both men and women make stem from misreading signals given off by appearance.

We all have the right to wear sexually provocative clothes, but it is harder to be seen in Second Circle if you are projecting a strong come-on. This tends to be a generalized Third Circle statement which announces sex, not intelligence. If you dress in this way, unenlightened men in a position of power will see you as trying to please them and turn them on. If such unenlightened men work for you, they will assume you have gained power through sex as opposed to your own skill. This will be most prominent in the minds of those who envy your position, including the women you are in charge of.

If you wear these clothes, be prepared for trouble. Staying in Second will alert you sooner to a problem and can even help others to see through the cosmetic quality of the clothes. However, don't expect much support from the people around you, particularly other women, if they feel you are in sexual competition with them.

The male and female form can still be celebrated in Second without being provocative—think about Michelangelo's *David* or Botticelli's *Venus*. Men and women can still dress in a way that celebrates their sex's physical shape and attributes. If you dress yourself with Second Circle awareness of the environment or person you are dressing for, then you can still have the freedom of personal expression through fashion without unwittingly provoking criticism.

Sexual Threats in Education

Really good teaching takes place in Second Circle, but this presence must be fueled by care and not sexual desire.

However tempting, no teacher should ever flirt with or harass a student. The teacher is spoiling that student's education and compromising the learning of others in the class.

The age of the student is irrelevant, as the central issue is one of misuse of power. Any calm examination of the sexual dynamics between teacher and student reveals a fundamental fact: the student wants to please the teacher and can therefore be prone to flirting. If you are a teacher in this situation, remember, it's not you they fancy, it's your power. If you feel that a student is encouraging you to flirt, withdraw. Don't be flattered—walk away, and don't allow yourself to be alone with the student.

Equally, students who feel that they are being groomed by a teacher should withdraw and avoid being alone with that teacher, showing no encouragement.

Sexual Threats in the Home

The worst form of abuse takes place in families, when the person who should be a child's prime protector turns into the predator.

Sexual or physical abuse of a child is obscene and will probably destroy the child's Second Circle energy and presence forever. Sometimes, even huge amounts of therapy later in life will not restore that former child's sense of trust and connection.

I recently taught a lady whose grandfather had sexually abused her from the age of four. Her mother, grandmother, and father all allowed this in a terrible conspiracy of silence. The grandfather was powerful and a great patriarchal figure. This courageous lady was pulling herself back into life forty years after the abuse. She smiled wryly and said to me, "Apart from anything else, do you know how much that abuse has cost me in therapy? I would just like my mother to know that."

Husbands batter wives; wives batter husbands; both generally stay in the relationship because they are battered into a dazed First Circle. However, the situation can also be more subtle.

Fathers and mothers may talk about their children's bodies in an overtly sexual way. Perhaps in its even more subtle form, fueled by some aspects of the media, there is a trend in parents to teach their children to flirt and then reward them for it. If this is done in an intense Second Circle, it is not only deeply confusing to the child, but the parent is also setting up their offspring to be a prime target for harassment later in life.

It is relatively easy to recognize physical and sexual abuse knocking us out of Second Circle. We know when the spoilers hit us in these ways, and we also know when we hit out and hurt others. It is less obvious when we meet intellectual, emotional, or spiritual spoilers of our presence.

Intellectual Threats

Intellectual abuse is often the brash Third Circle dismissal of your intelligence that doesn't even consider your point of view. It can also be the more subtle First Circle rolling of the eyes, which ridicules your ideas. Ferocious intellectual tyrants will make an all-out Second Circle attack on someone less educated or empowered than themselves. This kind of attack is fair game among equals, but it is the equivalent of a mugging when it intellectually flattens a less well equipped person. Think of the following people, and imagine the impact of their comments on the recipient.

Telltale Signs of Intellectual Abuse

The husband who publicly calls his wife stupid
The wife who publicly scoffs at her husband's views
The parents who deny their children's opinions
The boss who constantly maintains no one knows better
than he/she
The teacher who can't be wrong

How to Parry Such Abuse

The only way to deal with intellectual abuse is to call it to order. Do this calmly, freely, and in Second Circle, with direct questions:

"Do you realize you have just dismissed my point of view?"
"Do you think I am unintelligent?"
"Do you always treat people this way?"

You might get some truthful and painful replies, but at least you will begin to know your enemy. This type of intellectual bully rarely gets challenged.

You may also find yourself in situations where a bully is attacking a friend or colleague and you then have a more complex decision to make. This is often the case at "civilized" dinner parties when a partner is attacking their other half. Do you stand up for the victim or not? Obviously, it is very difficult to do, but you should stay connected in Second with the victim, without necessarily needing to vocalize your support.

You must be aware of the danger and recognize that if anyone insults you they are trying to reduce you.

If you respond to an insult in Third, you will heighten the exchange and it can get out of control. A response in First is weak; you have lost and they will strike again. Stay in a calm Second. If the insult is given in First or Third, then you might disarm your attacker by asking them, in Second, to repeat the insult. Try to get them to say it in Second. Don't back down. If they continue, you might try to talk calmly to them in Second, but if that is impossible don't feel ashamed to leave—in Second.

If you are clearly in Second when responding to an insult, at least it has been witnessed and the speaker hasn't fully got away with it. In other words, the person knows what they have done and is aware that their bile has been witnessed.

Emotional Threats

Emotional abuse is often more subtle than the intellectual form, but how familiar is this litany of emotional abuse?

- "You don't feel that . . . I feel more than you . . . I haven't hurt you . . . I don't care what you feel."
- "I apologize but will do it again."
- "I apologize but won't change my behavior."
- "Don't cry . . . grow up . . . boys don't cry . . . your feelings embarrass me."

Emotional spoilers appear in all the above comments.

I would suggest that if you deal intimately in Second with your partner, friends, children, and colleagues, you wouldn't say any of these things. This is because you will have an acute and exact awareness of their emotional distress and whether that distress is real or not. Most such remarks are only communicated to you when the speaker is blocking your feelings in Third Circle, or else not even bothering to deal with the feeling, in a casual and uncaring First Circle. When delivered to you in either Third or First Circle, draw the person into Second Circle with you and ask them if they really mean to hurt you, and whether they are prepared to repeat the remark in Second Circle. If you do receive these remarks in Second, they will constitute abuse. To put it simply, you have proved that they want to hurt you.

This lack of care adds up to emotional abuse, and its recognition could well signal the end of an unhealthy relationship.

Spiritual Threats

Not all threats are physical or even emotional. They may take the form of attacking our belief systems and our personal experiences of the divine or the supernatural.

Some years ago, I lived in a house that was haunted. The ghost lived on the top floor, and I would meet him on the staircase and in the top bedroom. Friends who slept up there would wake up to find him shaking them. I even met a doctor who had lived in the house some years before me and had also met this fellow.

One day a friend brought one of his colleagues around for tea. The subject of the ghost came up. This man, who I had never met before, smirked and tutted in First Circle and then in Third Circle.

"I don't believe in ghosts." He grinned. "I would never see your ghost."

I replied, "Perhaps you wouldn't, but are you suggesting that I haven't seen this ghost?"

Pause.

"Yes." His chest rose and he went further into Third Circle.

"So you are saying that the experience I have had in this house is not real because you wouldn't have that experience?"

"Yes."

"Let me get this straight. You are right and I am wrong. Your experience of life is more valid than mine."

Pause. He changed the subject.

The point is that it is spiritual tyranny for anyone to tell anyone else what they should or should not believe. Faith and a connection to the divine through unconditional love combine to create a personal experience and a freedom that no one has the right to challenge. Nobody deserves to kill or be killed for their faith.

21

Witnessing the Damage

We all want to be known. Simply said, we want to be witnessed in life. None of us wants to leave life without being noticed, and witnessing and being noticed are Second Circle activities.

A character in the play called *The Government Inspector* by Gogol simply explores this profound human desire. Bobchinsky waits patiently for hours to meet a government inspector from St. Petersburg, believing he knows and is intimate with the Tsar of Russia. He wishes to petition the Inspector to tell the Tsar that in such-and-such a town in such-and-such a province in Russia lives a man called Bobchinsky. His desire is simply to be witnessed by his ruler.

This Second Circle recognition by a leader is why big organizations work better when the CEO knows and talks to the rest of the staff. A Second Circle acknowledgment of the security guard or cleaner makes for a better and more productive work environment.

However, it is equally important to all of us that any abuse is witnessed by others. We need the damage and pain that we have experienced to be spoken by ourselves or others in Second Circle. This is why miscarriages of justice are felt so keenly by the victims. In the courtroom, a victim waits for the perpetrator of the crime to apologize. When the law fails them, their pain is that much worse.

It is so important for you to voice your damage in Second Circle and for it to be received in Second Circle. That exchange can heal. Often we have to perform this exchange with a therapist or even a priest, but such witnessing can only satisfy if we manage it in Second Circle and it is received in the same energy. It is equally essential that others witness wrongs committed against you. What a relief it is when you hear someone defend you and acknowledge the injustice done to you. In South Africa, when apartheid was finally abolished, this need was formalized by organized sessions of reconciliation between victims and their perpetrators.

It is crucial for you to remember that even if you are unable to defend someone as they are being attacked, you should at least witness it later to the victim in Second Circle.

> I once witnessed the most savage verbal attack performed by a famous playwright on an innocent member of the front of house staff at a theatre. I was not alone—the director of the play and the artistic director of the theatre were also present, and I am afraid none of us stepped in to defend the poor girl. I felt so ashamed that I found her the next day and we talked. When I felt she was fully present to me, I apologized for not helping her and clearly stated that the playwright was out of order. She was immensely relieved, as the eloquence of the attack made her believe that she must have done something wrong.

Here are three other stories that underscore my point that our pain and humiliation need to be witnessed.

> A very brilliant actor told me that her uncle had systematically raped her between the ages of five and eleven. He was a general in the army, and her family lived with him and his wife after her father's death. She, of course, had the added

responsibility that her family was reliant on the uncle's hospitality. As she aged, her need to say something and witness the wrong done to her grew. Eventually, in her late thirties, she found herself in his living room with the family, drinking dry sherry. The garden doors were open and it was a beautiful English summer evening. Suddenly, she got a rare moment to be alone with him. He had wandered into the garden and she followed. She described the moment as feeling completely connected to him. He turned and looked at her, and they made deep eye contact.

Calmly, without rage, she said, "I remember what you did to me."

She was in absolute Second Circle.

He gasped and went ashen with fear as my friend just turned away and left him with his actions witnessed. She says that in that moment she was completely unburdened and that his abuse finished destroying her. She had finally witnessed it. Now, with complete focus, she was able to move on.

I heard a similar story from a black South African actor. He had been tortured throughout apartheid, and after the government's fall he would sometimes meet his torturer in the street. This, of course, was always a difficult encounter. The torturer looked guilty and no one knew the protocol. How do you meet your customized abuser?

Then, one day, when he felt that he was really in the moment, the actor saw his torturer and stopped him. He saw fear in the other man's eyes, but he also knew that the torturer was present. The actor took a breath and said directly to the man, "I was right and you were wrong."

With this he moved on down the street, leaving behind the bewildered man and some of the pain of his abuse.

I am willing to wager that it would have been easier for the torturer to be verbally or physically abused in Third Circle than to have this truth told in Second Circle.

Many years ago, I was working with a well-known actor on a show. The director was known to be vile and abusive, particularly toward women. During early rehearsals the director found a weak woman and started to bully her. At first it was the occasional remark, but this began to escalate into a full-scale personality assassination.

The director was very influential, so although the rest of the company was uneasy, no one wished to risk their career by defending the unfortunate actor. We all felt ashamed, but also relief that "she's getting it, not me." This is a syndrome and energy attached to many scenarios where a group witnesses a powerful bully in action.

Then a miracle happened. The actor got to his feet and in clear Second Circle, without raising his voice, said to the director, "I will not tolerate you speaking to this actress in that way."

Silence. The director clocked and received the challenge. He turned and walked out of the rehearsal, never to return. A cheer went up amongst the cast. That action is one of the reasons why I will love this actor forever.

Some people will always try to spoil your Second Circle energy, but you are more easily healed if that destruction is faced, met, and voiced in Second Circle.

22

Technology

I am slipping into what might seem a strange section here. Technology doesn't set out to spoil us, but it does potentially betray us and our Second Circle presence if we do not handle it with care. We believe it is there to help our lives, but if we are not careful it can deprive us of our life force.

Technology can be and often is the most solid barrier between you and others. It is doing an important job for you, but it can also cut you off from the person on the other side of the technology. Here is an example of a technological barrier that most of us have experienced. You go out for a meal with someone you really want to talk to, and they spend most of the time taking calls on their cell phone and receiving or sending texts on their BlackBerry. The result is that you feel that an instrument designed to make communication finer is actually destroying connections between people. A phone has become more important than you. If questioned, the offender often seems shocked as they are only "keeping in touch."

Computers

E-mails can sound unintentionally rude and stark to the receiver. The person writing them isn't aware of you, but is "keeping in touch" without acknowledging anyone at the other end. When you write e-mails, try to do it in Second Circle with people in mind. The trouble comes when you dash one off in Third Circle or have a self-centered communication in First Circle. If it is an important or sensitive message, read it back aloud in Second Circle before you send it. In this way you will become aware if it is too stark. People who spend hours on the computer can develop a Second Circle connection to a machine and fail to engage fully with the world. Even if you are doing great and creative Second Circle work on the computer, it is easy to wander around in a First Circle daze after leaving the technology behind.

After you have finished using your computer, get back into your Second Circle body and breathe. Perhaps walk with energy or pace around the room before rejoining the world. Look around and get Second Circle focus on objects in the space. Try to have a Second Circle conversation with someone, even if that just means a chat with the person you buy your coffee from.

All of this also applies to hours of watching TV or listening to music through headphones. Although you are probably intimately connected to the TV show and the music, you have to consciously rejoin the world if you want to maintain Second Circle energy.

Telephones

It is easy to not be in Second on the telephone, but you and others do know when this is happening. We have all experienced talking on the phone to someone and being aware when their attention has gone. Maybe they have placed their Second Circle energy onto a computer screen or are reading a newspaper, but it is definitely not on you.

Any good telesales person knows this and sells in Second Circle over the phone. In fact, if you want to politely rid yourself of their call, you wait for a moment when their focus falters and then finish the call. Bad telephone salespeople work in a frenzied Third Circle. If they manage to make a sale, it is because they have worn you down and you give up. You win sales in Second Circle just as you win computer games with that energy.

Remember, when you have an important call to make, always do it in Second Circle. Breathe to the receiver and envisage the person you are speaking to. If you don't know them, give them some form in your head—just knowing their name helps. Sit up or stand. It is even a good idea to place yourself in Second before dialing.

You will probably notice when you go into Third on the telephone—that is the moment when the listener holds the receiver away from their ear. In First, you completely disengage them and they will wander off, look out of the window, or rearrange their desk. You can't see them, so they are free to abandon you in whatever way they choose.

Microphones

The biggest mistake you can make with any presentation involving a microphone is thinking that it will do the energy work for you. All a microphone does is amplify the energy you offer.

If you are in First Circle, the microphone will heighten this lack of energy and your dullness will actually be communicated in a more alarming way. If you push into Third Circle with a microphone, you become more invulnerable and forceful. In this way you might sound unassailable, but you will not be heard or really understood. So, bear these techniques in mind if you have to use a microphone.

There are many sorts of microphones, each needing a different Second Circle technique. The radio-mike is attached to you and you carry a pack. Be aware that both the attachment and the pack can pull you into First Circle. The microphone's connection to your body and the presence of the pack inhibit your stance, making your body and breath withdraw. You must stay in Second Circle throughout your body, breath, and voice and stay connected by breathing to your audience. The mike will then boost your Second Circle energy rather than pull you back into First. The physical impediments of the microphone can also make you push into Third Circle, and that, as you know by now, is offputting.

A hand or stand microphone can prove more complex. You must maintain a Second Circle contact with the audience but only breathe to the mike. If you breathe beyond the mike, you will have too much energy and sound Third Circle. If you breathe only halfway to the mike, you will sound First Circle.

On radio, connect to the microphone in Second Circle body, breath, and voice, and then imagine that you are addressing an individual through the microphone.

The same applies to cameras. Breathe, speak, and humanize the lens in Second Circle. You will have to split Second Circle if you are speaking to someone on camera; that is, Second Circle with the person you are speaking to and also Second Circle with the camera.

Stage Lighting

Lighting helps the audience to see you on stage and gives you enormous importance. But the problem with advanced lighting is that it can mean that you can't see your audience—this isn't conducive to Second Circle connection, as you are strangely floundering around in the dark, despite the lights. If you know you are to be lit, get into the space without the lighting and feel the breath you need to fill the space. Check on where your eyeline should be, so that when lit you can breathe and look beyond the lights to the perimeter of the room or auditorium. This way the light illuminates you but doesn't close you down.

Travel

I am placing travel within this chapter as most travel is driven by technology. Even a few decades ago, the activity of traveling would jolt you into Second Circle. Travel was an adventure, and often dangerous. Adventures and dangers naturally require our survival presence.

The danger of travel is a given in Chaucer's *Canterbury Tales*. The pilgrims gathered to travel together as the ways were treacherous. In the company of strangers, the travelers told their stories.

Closer to our time and within living memory are journeys on foot over rough ground which would place anybody in Second Circle. People walked sometimes ten to fifteen miles a day to get to and from work, and in those walks there would be inevitable joy and comfort in meeting a stranger and passing the time of day with them in Second Circle. If you were lucky enough to own a horse and cart, you would have to be in Second Circle to ride or to steer the cart. I know there are stories about the horse knowing its way home when the master was drunk, but generally you need presence to be with a horse. Riding in carriages or stagecoaches was a bumpy business, as they had little or no suspension. If nothing else kept you in Second Circle, the bumps on the road would. Seas tossed the traveler aboard ship and kept them alert as shipwrecks happened on a very regular basis. The same is true of the early trains and planes. The persistent chug of a steam train might lull you for moments, but its sway and whistle keeps you alert.

Traveling was an adventure—the people encountered on the way, the passionate exchanges travel allowed, and the curiosity fueled by new places all served to keep the traveler in Second Circle.

How different it is today. The thought of another plane or train journey produces a First Circle yawn. Ships are built to make passengers feel they are on dry land. Only the fiercest seas make them rock. We know where we are going; there are so many people on the journeys we make that we don't really want to have to speak to them and only make contact if something very unusual happens. On planes or trains, many of us want to space out in First Circle and not have conversations with fellow passengers; but you will get better service from flight attendants and train inspectors if you speak to them in Second Circle.

Most airports and train stations look similar all over the world and the only points of interest are the shops and restaurants. We don't generally walk to travel, only for recreation, so there is no urgency in the walk.

Driving

Cars kill too many people because drivers are not in Second Circle. Of course, there are deaths when pedestrians or cyclists lose their survival energy, but mostly it is the car drivers who feel safe and isolated enough in their metal boxes not to pay full attention to the road. It is possible to feel alone and protected in a car and unaware of the force you have.

Aggressive and dangerous drivers are in Third Circle. The dithering, scared, and flustered ones are in First. If you are a passenger with either of these drivers, you should feel you have every right to ask them to stop and let you get out of the car.

Good driving is only possible in Second Circle, which is why anything that takes your Second Circle concentration off the road is dangerous, whether it is drink, talking on the telephone, or having an animated conversation with a passenger. Even eating or listening too intently to the radio can draw your Second Circle energy away from your driving.

Road rage starts with a string of Third Circle aggressions thrown at another vehicle without recognizing the driver's humanity. The heat of the exchange grows to a point when it can spill over into a vicious Third Circle attack.

To encourage better driving and safety on the streets, stay in Second Circle as you drive. If you make a mistake, acknowledge it and apologize in Second Circle. A wave will do. Give way. When possible allow other cars, bicycles, and pedestrians right of way. Make Second Circle contact with the driver, cyclist, or pedestrian. When you are helped in this way as a pedestrian or cyclist, thank in Second Circle. When you travel in taxis, the driver will drive better if greeted in Second. Bus drivers have a very lonely and often difficult job, particularly if they work in urban centers. A pleasant Second Circle acknowledgment of their existence will make their life more enjoyable.

Bicycles and motorcycles must be ridden well and safely in Second Circle energy to avoid First and Third Circle drivers. Cyclists will harm pedestrians if they aren't in Second Circle, and will damage or kill themselves if they don't negotiate the other traffic in Second. It is beyond ridiculous when you see cyclists listening to music on an iPod going around the busiest roundabouts in London, New York, or Los Angeles.

If you are traveling in a daze, reconnect when you reach your destination. Don't let the journey completely deenergize you.

23

Events
That
Spoil

Alongside the people who spoil our lives are the events that cause us to lose our presence.

Panic, Stress, and Trauma

My joyful son Michael came home from his nursery school one day inconsolable. He had taken his favorite toy to nursery and lost it. In that loss of a favorite toy lie all the clues to the pain that creates stress, panic, and trauma.

Where was the toy? Did the toy miss him? Had the toy been destroyed or, even worse, had some other child stolen it? Was that child now playing with Michael's toy?

All these questions were unanswerable, but the lack of answers just added to his distress. I remembered a pink ball that I lost at his age—three and a half—and all that distress returned for me, too.

Michael hasn't yet met other events that will bring him tears, but they will all bring about reactions similar to that at the loss of his toy: the loss of intimacy with a lover; the death of a loved one; the unsolved disappearance of a close friend or relative; someone else playing with an ex.

Michael's lost toy was a typical loss of innocence, which often results in a loss of Second Circle presence. We need to bring ourselves back from the trauma of loss if we don't want to live without our powerful life force. After any such pain, we have to relight the flame of our energy.

On a practical level, you must learn to identify the physical effects of these emotions and seek help in making basic physical readjustments.

The first physical signs of stress and panic occur in the body and breath. Whatever is throwing you into this turmoil, through your mind and heart, will manifest directly in physical signals that can be seen in others and felt in yourself. Panic pulls the breath up into the body, probably in an attempt to brace yourself against the world. This is a classic Third Circle manifestation. In extreme examples, the body becomes so rigid that the breath locks in the upper chest. You can't breathe at all and are actually facing death! In panic, the effects are vivid and unavoidable, and you therefore know you have a problem.

Stress has similar physical effects but is harder to monitor and can take years to build up in your body and breath. Actually, as soon as you adopt a Third Circle posture, you are moving closer toward panic, stress, and loss of your authentic self.

If you don't return to Second from these periods of stress you will, one day, either explode or implode. Imploding means detaching yourself from the source of the panic or stress and falling into First Circle. In this way you actually give up, having become too tired of holding up a front and denying the pain. You surrender.

The arrival of trauma into your life, body, and breath can be so painful and harsh that the only way you can survive is through First Circle. You retreat from the world to lick your wounds and heal. This retreat is understandable, if it isn't permanent; but if you never reemerge after examining the pain in First, you will slowly fade away.

This trapped (First) or exploding (Third) energy can explain why, when you are under stress, panicked, or severely shocked, other people's energy impinges on yours. In these states you bump into people on the street, get clumsy with objects or people, and in extreme cases attract the attention of muggers or foul-mouthed abuse from strangers. The weak pick up on your weakness and disconnection.

Here is a list of Third Circle panic and stress signs:

- Shoulders rising
- Jaw clenching
- Upper chest lifting and bracing
- Stomach tightening
- Hands clenching
- Breath shallow and locked into the upper chest
- Gasping for breath
- Topping up breath and having an insufficient outward breath
- A fast exchange of air that results in not enough oxygen, which in turn sparks greater panic as you are actually drowning in carbon dioxide
- Flickering eyes
- A tight, pushed, higher-pitched voice

First Circle detachment includes:

- Rounding of shoulders
- Drooping head
- Looking down
- Slumped spine
- Over-released stomach

- A sighing breath that can stop for long periods of time as you refuse to breathe and take the life force of oxygen. When you do breathe, it is very slight, with little movement in the body.
- Dead eyes
- A flat, dull, and falling voice

Returning to Second Circle

After any trauma, you must return to Second Circle presence. Therapists can guide you differently and successfully; but in Circle work, there are two ways of working yourself out of these states.

Everyone, at some point in their lives, will experience panic, stress, or trauma. There is no shame in these feelings and no weakness attached to them. The important initial stage is to honor the feelings without the humiliation that often accompanies your distress.

A denial of these feelings will trap you in them and weaken the rest of your life. A light will go out and you will feel helpless and pessimistic. You will lose joy. Any concentration on the world outside you helps to relieve this distress. The whole energy of Second is to focus outside yourself—this can help to alleviate your internal despair.

Discipline yourself to look at and listen to the world in Second:

As you look and listen, breathe to the sound and point of visual focus.

Listen actively to calm music.

Visit nature, and look and listen to the sights and sounds around you.

Look and breathe to the stars and the moon.

Look and breathe over the sea or a lake, mountains and hills.

Listen and breathe to birdsong, the surge of the sea, rain falling, the wind.

Take a holiday—this not only helps you rest but engages you
in new surroundings to look at and listen to in Second.

If you can't take a holiday, visit a park, a zoo, or an
aquarium.

Visit art galleries; go to a classical concert or the theatre;
and look, listen, and breathe in Second.

Here are some exercises that offer physical solutions:

• Stand and center in Second Circle, releasing the shoulders,
knees, stomach, and jaw. Keep the spine up but not rigid
and the chest open, not lifted or depressed. Breathe low,
calmly, and silently in your body. Keep your voice open.
Voice your concerns. Speak to an object or pet in Second
Circle out loud about your panic, stress, or trauma.

• Walk with Second Circle energy, if possible over rough
ground.

• Exercise in Second Circle.

• Shower and breathe in Second Circle.

• Prepare a meal and eat in Second Circle.

• Meet friends and talk to them in Second.

Boredom

Boredom, surprisingly, can kill just as easily as urban anxiety
and stress.

When you are bored, you fall into First Circle and become
more and more self-obsessed. You are prone to detachment and
are attracted to activities that seem to jolt you alive again—
maybe the quick fix of drink, casual sex, fast cars, even violence. Most of these activities are probably in Third Circle and
therefore don't really click you back into your presence.

The one thing that will help is to move out from First or Third into Second Circle. People in a state of boredom seem to wait in First for others to help them out of their grayness. Only you can help yourself, and if you are not in Second you won't realize when others are trying to help you.

Remember, Second Circle is a place of giving and taking. If you are taking without giving in First, you will get bored and life will seem pointless.

Many years ago, I taught a group of very privileged young women. It was one of the most depressing jobs I have ever had—much harder than teaching in a prison. These women had everything and yet offered nothing to the world. They sat and waited to be entertained, openly yawning at me and their peers.

I tried everything to engage them. The establishment was a London "finishing school" and they were supposed to be learning how to speak "nicely"—to eventually support their super-rich husbands.

In despair, I challenged them in this way. I said I would spend five minutes talking to them about how I found them as a class, and then they could reply and tell me what they thought of me as a teacher. I grant this was a desperate and dangerous tactic.

What I said to them went something like this: "I hope you all get what you want in life. Husband, beautiful children, country house, town mansion, shopping trips to Paris, New York, and London. Travel far and wide and stay in the most glamorous resorts on the planet . . . But beyond this, I believe you will still be bored, because in order to feel alive you have to give, and I have never seen any of you give anything to anyone in my presence."

After I finished, there was a shocked silence. The Alpha female then spoke up: "You don't bore us."

My reply was, "Then why don't you believe you should show anything, give, offer? Do you really think you can go through life showing nothing?"

Another silence.

No one had ever challenged them, and their privilege had cocooned them from ever having to move out beyond themselves and offer in Second Circle. They seemed doomed to a life of boredom.

It occurs to me that this insidious curse of privilege is thoroughly explored by Shakespeare. Those who seemingly have everything have to lose belongings, power, and love in order to feel their humanity. All his privileged characters undergo tests which help them learn to give and to respond to life in Second Circle. These tests ensure that they finally learn to face life with presence and gravitas. Gravitas is not a doomed place but one that has a counterpoint of joy. It is the endless pursuit of trivia that will destroy you and your presence.

24
Heightened Emotional Release

There is another sure way of reconnecting yourself after the deadening effects of harsh emotional pain. This is commonly referred to as "release."

Release is unquestionably good. An abandoned laugh is good for you, as is a good cry, or a wail in grief. A scream is the appropriate response to fear. All of these releases use massive amounts of breath and energy, and the principle of uninhibited sound leaving you is simple: the oxygen and sounds purge you. The energy of an emotion is projected out of you, and you feel better. The movement and energy is emotion—note the word "emotion," motion—unleashed from your body.

The act of breathing through and releasing sound with feeling challenges and frequently overcomes your habitual First or Third blocks and controls, and that freeing places you back in Second Circle. The strength of the release returns you to your natural Second Circle presence.

The power of these releases can draw a First Circle person out of themselves and blow the mask of a Third Circle person away—you are being cleansed of your pain and brought back to life.

Perhaps you have noticed that if mourners allow tears or wailing in their grief, their faces clear. The Second Circle mourners are the ones who have openly released. They are actively living their grief.

Compare that clarity with the First Circle mourners, who detach and go inward as a result of their grief. There is no release, only a terrible emotional constipation. Third Circle mourners are on the verge of or actually in hysteria. The release is not specific and is being played out in chaos.

When you mourn in Second Circle, you suddenly see the world clearly, and this offers comfort. The grief allows you to see other people's grief and know that the road you are traveling is occupied by other individuals. So many of us have been taught to rationalize our emotions and box them in, and stoically encouraged not to show feelings but to control them. Of course, controls are necessary, but it is also necessary to feel the freedom of release when justified. Release is healthy and unburdens you.

When you allow yourself actively to cry, scream, or swear, this can be an effective release of anger in Second Circle. A First Circle cry chokes you up and implodes the pain within you. A Third Circle cry can release some pain but will make you push, so that it sounds manufactured. A Second Circle scream can scare off a mugger. A First Circle one will pull energy into you and weaken you, and a Third Circle one is a noticeable bluff.

Release into Second Circle

To achieve a Second Circle cry, place the sound out of you to a specific point (howling to the moon!) and recognize the specific source of your pain. Is it physical, emotional, or spiritual? An impassioned Second Circle cry to a god or goddess is a very good release. When you want to release a feeling, try to remind yourself of these basic principles:

- Stand in center and breathe as low as you can.
- Feel the breath's readiness.

- Pushing against a wall will help, as will energized pacing, as long as you keep the breath low.
- Keep the throat open by imagining a yawn and then place any sound out of you.
- Don't push or swallow the sound.
- An *ah* is a sound that allows emotions to release.

You can do this release lying on your back, but be careful that gravity doesn't let the sound fall back into you.

A Second Circle release clearly tells you when the pain, fear, and anger are overspent—something you cannot experience in First or Third. In First, it cannot be over because it's trapped in you; in Third, it's so pushed and generalized you cannot gauge when you are spent and released. The pain goes on beyond its natural life and burdens you beyond its real power.

Try this. Next time you want to swear, do it in Second Circle. After a few expletives, you'll feel better and won't need to go on. The anger and frustration have dispersed and been placed out of you. A Second Circle curse works because it is aimed at a particular person and can therefore be really dangerous. Swear in First Circle and you will savage *yourself* with sound, not the object of your distress. Third Circle swearing is general and never hits the true mark, so you have to keep on pushing and swearing!

Now think about laughter. In many societies, laughing is the only socially acceptable expression of feeling allowed. Therefore, laughter is not always an expression of joy. It fulfills and releases other emotions. It may mock and ridicule. It can express fear, embarrassment, humiliation, scorn, even grief.

True Laughter

We all know exactly what is meant by a particular type of laughter—be it your own or one that is aimed at you. When these laughs are hiding or perverting the true feeling behind them, they are rarely in Second Circle, but tend to be hidden in First or manufactured in Third Circle. Consequently, these laughs and the hidden meanings underneath are hard to challenge as they are not directed at you. Beware if malice is expressed in a full Second Circle laugh as you are really dealing with a sadist.

True laughter is an outpouring of joy that engages the whole body, breath, voice, and face. It is beautifully expressed in the images of the laughing Buddha. This laughter crosses cultures, travels through time, and unites humanity. It is near impossible to hate someone you can laugh with, let alone hurt them. When you laugh with someone, you become equal and at one with each other. A smile in Second unites you; a laugh forges your spirits together and transcends race, age, religion, and class.

Laughing with joy might start in First or Third, but if it grows and builds in you it draws you into Second Circle and is the voice of your own angel, the sound of your full, naked, unpretentious, and loving being. When someone laughs with joy, you will see their presence. After your own laughter, you will be seen and see the world in Second Circle.

A good laugh bonds relationships: if you cease to laugh in a relationship that was once full of joyful laughter, then you know that the relationship is in trouble. Laugh with your children and they will always come home to you. Laugh with your employees, not at them, and they will work hard and loyally for you. Laugh with tragedy and it will not defeat you. Hence the saying, "to see the funny side of life." Survivors laugh.

If you mostly live in Second Circle, you will be able to laugh joyfully with yourself and others. But First or Third Circle livers are sometimes choked off from this natural joy.

Some people have really lost the ability to laugh freely in Second Circle and the joy has dried up. If you suspect you fall into this category, the joy can be rediscovered as the inability to laugh fully is connected to control and your fear of full presence.

It is particularly important that you do the body and breath exercises described in previous chapters. By doing them and staying in Second Circle, you might find your laughter. When you do, you are likely to move from laughter into tears of grief and fear as you rediscover the full range of your emotions.

Joyful laughter is easier with others, so gravitate to harmless activities where children laugh. A children's show with children laughing can activate even the most cynical adult into laughter, particularly if that adult stays in Second with the activity, breathes in Second, and remains non-judgmental.

Group Exercise

Here's a group exercise that can produce the most wonderful abandoned laughter. You will need about seven people—the more the merrier!

- Lie on your back in a circle, placing your head on the stomach of the person to your right.
- Arrange yourselves so that eventually everyone has their head on someone's stomach and someone else's head on their own stomach.
- All breathe, relax the shoulders, and start gently vocalizing a *ha ha ha*. Keep it going and you will gradually experience full-throttle laughter that can go on for minutes.

At the end of the exercise you will feel released, bonded, exhausted, and present with each other in Second Circle.

Part
Two

Living
with Full
Presence

I have spent the greater part of this book exploring ways for you to get into your Second Circle energy, as well as the many forces that deprive you of that power. Now is the time to look at how you can maintain that energy and stay living within it.

Most of us have families and communities, most of us have to work, and most of us hopefully find time to play.

In some professions, Second Circle is essential to the way people work. You cannot be a successful performer or athlete without presence. If you have ambition to move up in the corporate world, you won't do so if you don't have presence. If you have chosen to work in the law, medicine, education, religion, or politics, you can operate to an extent without Second Circle but shouldn't.

If you don't work in any of the above professions, you can rarely get through life without meeting policemen, lawyers, doctors, teachers, priests, or politicians. In short, you need to know how to place these people in Second Circle if they are not already there. These professions control people's lives, and if the professionals are not working with positive presence they can be destroyed by their careers.

Families, communities, and relationships are enormous subjects, so I can only offer snapshots that will hopefully illuminate and help you explore all of your life.

> It is required you do awake your faith.
> —WILLIAM SHAKESPEARE, THE WINTER'S TALE

25

Families

But the child's sob curseth deeper in the silence
Than the strong man in his wrath!

—Elizabeth Barrett Browning,
"Cry of the Children"

A baby cries out. It is frightened, hungry, dirty, or cold. The baby wants comfort, a parent and some human contact, an adult's strength, power, and protection. The initial call is in Second Circle, and expects and deserves a Second Circle response. If there is no response, the cry will get more distraught and desperate, and will move into Third Circle. If there is still no response, the baby will withdraw into a detached First Circle.

Many babies now in Western society in a hectic age sleep alone and unanswered. There are even baby-rearing manuals that encourage parents not to respond and let the baby cry. It is a strange society that ignores its children yet constantly demands service.

The unanswered cry is harmless if it happens rarely; but if a Second Circle cry goes unanswered enough times, the baby will feel disconnected from the world and become detached in First. After all, why bother calling out if no one comes. The other reaction is to move into a Third Circle energy that demands attention but becomes so enraged that the baby won't feel anyone else's presence.

A human cry for help should be answered; that is what we all need and desire. But it has to start in the family during those initial months and years. A genuine cry, which is natural for a baby, should have a genuine response. Is that too much to ask? The parent won't become the baby's slave, which is the parent's fear. Actually, it is the unanswered call that will eventually come back to haunt parents and society.

If appropriately answered, the baby will stop crying out, knowing its needs will be met. In this way babies develop confidence and self-esteem, which allow them to stay present to and in the world. Confidence is a manifestation of entitlement and entitlement starts with the answered call.

It's the detached child or the overdemanding child who is a burden on the parents. Some baby-rearing techniques in the West are producing children and young people who are either detached in First or have so much rage about going unanswered and unnoticed that they erupt into Third Circle aggressive behavior. It is the right of every baby and child to feel the parent's full Second Circle attention that is filled with unconditional love.

> Behold the Child among his newborn blisses,
> A six years' Darling of a pygmy size!
> See, where 'mid work of his own hand he lies,
> Fretted by sallies of his mother's kisses,
> With light upon him from his father's eyes!
>   —WILLIAM WORDSWORTH,
>   "Ode on Intimations of Immortality"

I know this sounds very simplistic, but I truly believe that a child will accept any boundaries and discipline if they are set with a positive presence of love communicated in Second Circle. These children can leave their home base as adults with the ease and knowledge that they have been loved unconditionally. They will want to return home and visit after their wanderings.

A child unacknowledged in Second Circle will do anything to be noticed, even if that parental attention comes with aggression instead of love. To the unnoticed child, the force of a parent's rage at least means they have had an effect on the adult, even though that effect is negative presence.

In the constant rush of everyday life, notice how unintentionally parents deal with their children in Third Circle: observe babies being shushed in Third, or sung and read to in Third; see how they are sent off to school, met at the school gates, and dragged around the supermarket in Third. Of course, there have to be times when Third is appropriate, as a child cannot always be the center of attention and also needs to be allowed to reflect in First.

Try some of these Second Circle exercises every day with your children, particularly at the beginning and end of their day, and whenever you meet and part. Begin to mark their lives with presence, love, and care. Use Second Circle eye contact, breathe to them, use an open Second Circle voice as much as possible, don't shout as it doesn't ever work, and always touch in Second.

The Child in Second Circle

- Nurse and comfort a baby in Second Circle. Wait until you feel the baby's breath tune in to Second Circle with your breath, before putting it back to sleep. In this way you will feel the baby's Second Circle connection to you and know when the fear has disappeared.
- Sing in Second Circle.
- Read children stories in Second Circle.
- Listen in Second, even while doing the dishes or preparing a meal.
- When reprimanding a child, stop what you are doing, turn the music down or the TV off, and get eye and touch contact with them. Breathe to them, and speak freely and clearly in Second Circle.
- Praise the child in Second Circle and tell them you love them in Second Circle.

Given the way we live in an era when both parents generally work, it is essential to carve out time every day for a Second Circle exchange—do this without any distractions, TV, or background noise. It might be helpful to establish a time that is still and silent before any exchange happens. Keep your breath calm and low in the body and speak with an open voice. If you push vocally or shout constantly, a child will shout back at you.

The ritual of a meal together and Second Circle communication can be very enjoyable. If you have to talk about negative aspects of the day or a child's behavior, balance the negativity with positive remarks. Listen to them in Second Circle.

A walk, hand-in-hand, is also productive for Second Circle conversation. Hold hands in Second Circle even if they are struggling not to! Ask their opinion in Second Circle, and don't belittle it but discuss whatever they say. Avoid talking about a child as though they are not there. This is particularly unpleasant if your comments are negative. Actively discourage other adults from doing this. If they want to find out your child's age, interests, and so on, make them ask your child directly in Second Circle.

Remember, a child with a new arrival on the scene will need extra helpings of Second Circle attention, even if it's from a grandparent or other relatives and friends. None of us likes being displaced and the only comfort is more presence from an adult. Set good examples by being in Second with your partner and family.

There are other important benefits involved in a daily check in Second Circle. If you make Second Circle contact with your child every day, you will notice when they are not able to make it with you. That is a sure sign that something is wrong in their life. Of course, they have the right to reflect in First Circle, but if they absent themselves from you in Second for long periods of time, then you must investigate what is happening to them. Some force or abuse is detaching them.

"Quality Time"

"Quality time" is a modern cliché, but it is essential. However, it can only be quality if you and the family are in Second Circle together. Holidays and outings can become family nightmares if you don't practice being in Second Circle together and recognize the pleasure you and your children are experiencing.

When you come home from a frustrating day at work, bring yourself back into Second before dealing with your family. On any journey, take time to make contact with your partner and children. In the car, help them notice the landscape outside, but do it in Second Circle. Talk about the train, the bus, the plane, and the surroundings. On every journey, even the regular school run, there is always something new to be explored together in Second Circle. Bus terminals, airports, and train stations are all places of rich present details that can be used to educate your child in Second Circle.

Approach every new experience for your children, such as a visit to the zoo, where new animals are seen for the first time, with positive presence. Castles, steam engines, baseball games should be locked into place in your child's mind by a moment between you and them in Second Circle.

All children will withdraw from their parents on a regular basis; it's part of their development. But that withdrawal only has meaning for them and you if it is noticed! This can only happen if you don't try to control them. Be sure to notice them regularly in Second Circle and welcome them back in Second Circle when they become attentive to you again.

Around School

Be present as you say good-bye to your children and meet them again after school. When they bring work home to you, examine it in Second Circle in front of them. Communicate with their teachers in Second Circle. The more you notice the teacher with presence, the more that teacher will be present to your child.

Know your child's friends in Second Circle, and not only will you spot bad influences more rapidly but also you will make your child feel safer in these friendships. If you suspect a child is bullying yours, talk to those concerned in Second Circle. Do so without intimidation: you will become real to the bully and the people involved and the right kind of power in their minds.

Support every endeavor by your child in Second Circle—artwork, athletic matches, school concerts or plays—even if it bores you or you fundamentally disapprove of the activity. If you are present to it, then a real discussion can occur. As an adult, you must stay present with children even if they are shouting at or insulting you. Stay present when they storm off. Leave present messages on their phones and write e-mails to them in Second Circle. Try not to discuss their culture—music, films, or fashion—especially if you hate it and before you have experienced it in Second Circle. Naturally they will want something different to your culture, but don't belittle their passions without knowledge of them.

> Don't limit a child to your own learning, for he was born in another time.   —RABBINICAL TEACHING

Stay present to them through their failures. They need you and your love more at these times. Any disapproval will make them feel more abandoned and deepen the wound.

The Spoiled Child

This is a fantastic phrase, because some children have indeed been spoiled by their parents and that spoiling when it grows out of control can seep into and destroy the rest of their life. By placing full attention on a child in Second Circle, you are not spoiling them. You are insisting that they stay present to you and the world: in so doing they will learn to respect and honor others.

A spoiled child believes he or she is more important than anyone else. Love and attention have been lavished on them without any demands being made, and in this way the child is not present to the rights of other people. A spoiled child has been given to without being taught to give back. The road is one-way.

In some ways it is easy and even lazy for a parent to give, give, give, without asking for attention back. Such giving can be through guilt that the parent hasn't had Second Circle time with the child. Mostly, the spoiling is a generalized Third Circle lavishing on a child. It is material loving, not present caring.

The parent is a guide, not a tyrant. Your child in Second Circle is an equal, not inferior to you, and relishes human attention from you. What's more, children like structure, not an abandoned freedom. This attention is more important to anyone than material gifts, or excessive amounts of food and treats that might occupy but never satisfy them. Maybe it's not immediately possible to be their friend. You are a loving guide. As long as boundaries are given in Second Circle, and are clear and reasoned with love, a child will understand. Children love order and reason; they respond to things that fit into place.

If you think about it, appropriate children's toys are concrete examples of order and place and provide endless fascination for young children. Different-shaped bricks fit into the appropriate holes. The patterns emerging in a kaleidoscope satisfy a sense of order. So do miniature representations of life, be they train sets, dollhouses, tea sets, or farmyards played with and ordered appropriately. At the end of the day, toys are often placed by the child in neat lines ready for the next day's adventures. Try telling a child a story that they know well and getting the order wrong. You won't be popular and they will make your error very clear to you!

Children have to break the boundaries and rules, but they will do so knowingly and then understand the consequences fully if these too are explained in Second Circle. We can all stomach justice if we know the rules, and if those rules are administered fairly.

As structures are set in place, a family pattern begins to emerge. Children can then learn about responsibility through clear and loving structures. This is the start of an initiation into responsible behavior which benefits all of us. It is how a child becomes an adult. Children cannot become adults unless they are present with responsible adults and elders and know they are acknowledged and respected by them. It is only possible to give and receive respect in Second Circle. You cannot shout for it in Third.

As children grow, they need to disconnect from their parents; but that shouldn't mean that the parents disconnect from them. It is extremely easy to stay present with children when they are pleasant and willing, but all children, particularly as they grow into adolescence, have phases of being unattractive. It is during these phases that it is essential for adults to stay with the younger, less experienced being. This is very hard and initially unrewarding, but it will save a child from fragmenting from you and from his or her roots.

Kids seek gangs for protection but also in order to feel connected and valued. Graffiti is an obvious way to be noticed and present on the streets as it is an expression of Second Circle territory-marking from kids desperate to be known in Second Circle.

It is not enough to be in the same space or house as your child. You have to *be there* with them, attentive, even when ignored and despised. The most troubled children need the most Second Circle attention, as it is the lack of that attention that has made them disturbed in the first place.

I remember teaching kids who had been thrown out of school

and dumped in a classroom together. As I entered the room, a wall of unpleasant and deeply unattractive energy hit me. They were unlikable, and their main study was how to make themselves more disliked by adults.

They expected me to dislike them. They didn't expect the non-judgmental attention of Second Circle care and reason. During every lesson I tried to stay with them, not be against them in Third. It was a titanic battle, but I won some of them over, and I discovered that underneath their rage of rejection and its escape into Third were frightened spirits, alone and lost, uncared for and therefore uncaring.

Without being present to and with them, I wouldn't have got past my disgust at their violence and disdain for society. They would have felt my disgust and it would have been easier for them to hate me. Some of them honored me with their real presence and consequently recognized my humanity. I wasn't just an uncool, judgmental woman, but a living person. During our first class, my handbag was stolen. Three weeks later, when the culprit had got to know me, I entered the classroom and found my bag and all its contents, except the money, lying on my desk. Its return was one of my greatest rewards in teaching.

When connections were made, we studied Shakespeare and Coleridge. I've always found that many of the most disruptive pupils are the brightest. Their intelligence makes them difficult, but not if they are recognized positively in Second Circle. Most of them had only received Second Circle fueled with rage and contempt.

Be there for your children—or you will lose them. If you feel you have already lost them, practice Second Circle with them and you will discover all is not lost, although you must still weather their inevitable and initial rejection of your attempts. A sure sign of mature behavior is the ability to stay in Second Circle with those you love, even through rejection. The rejecters will come home if their homecoming is noticed in Second.

The Family Meal

It's a family lunch. A subject is brought up by the rebelling adolescent which the head of the family doesn't wish to discuss over the meal—or most likely not at all. The adolescent could deliver the topic in an aggressive Third Circle, a piercing Second Circle, or a cynical First Circle. The good response would be to stay with them in Second, listen, discuss the topic, or assure them that you will do so later. The bad and more usual response is either to ignore the remark in First, in the belief that the rest of the family will follow your lead, or to use an aggressive Third to change the subject or start a shouting match always conducted in Third—and if these tactics fail, to silence the rebellion by sending the child to their room.

In my family, this was the routine. When I brought up unwelcome subjects, my father withdrew into First Circle, which could last for days. Like many men of his generation, he felt he didn't have to discuss anything that made him uncomfortable. My mother kept going by adopting an overcheerful Third Circle, changing the subject to how badly she had cooked the lamb and kicking me under the table in an attempt to silence me.

A friend's father used the more sophisticated technique of introducing a new subject of supreme dullness, such as a new route into work, which he spoke about in such detail in Third Circle that everyone was silenced—including any potential rebels in the ranks—by being bored stiff.

Children and Parents

As you read this book, you might be the child who knows that you have never had a satisfactory Second Circle relationship with your parents or parent. You might even be facing the thought of their death and fearful that you may never connect with them.

How do you break the mold? Begin to shake hands or hug them in Second Circle. I began hugging my mother in Second Circle in my early twenties. I made this decision when I discovered that she had lost two boyfriends in the war—one was killed three days before peace was declared. She lived through a war and obviously saw the poster telling the nation to "Keep calm and carry on." It struck me that for her, the risk of intimacy must be costly—it was connected to death.

She responded by hugging me back and we had years of great hugs. It was the last thing I did for her. I got onto her deathbed with her, and held her.

Try to get Second Circle eye contact with a parent. Seek out topics of conversation that interest them and engage in these topics. Notice if there are certain physical configurations that make them feel more relaxed and render it easier for them to be in Second Circle with you. This could be while you are watching TV or driving with them in the car. As you notice these situations, invest in them.

A dear friend of mine finally made contact with his father when he discovered he could speak to him in Second on country walks. They began by discussing cloud formations. His father's passion was the weather—something that my friend knew from childhood but only used forty years later as a doorway into their relationship.

Avoid time with them in situations that make them feel uncomfortable and disengage further. Note their habitual Circle. Are your parents present with each other? Do they have friends who have their full attention? These small efforts will make your time with a parent richer. They might notice your effort and respond actively in Second Circle with you. You might make real contact and begin to build an important relationship with them.

If they can't respond then, at least you've tried. You can continue to try even to the end, and if you love them, you will just have to take courage and tell them so in Second Circle. Even if they are in a coma and dying, our hearing (as I mentioned in the first section) is the last sense to fade, so they will die hearing you express your love for them. And that will free both them and you.

26

Relationships, Marriage, and Sex

Love is the difficult realization that
something other than oneself is real.

—Iris Murdoch

We are social animals and we all seek intimate Second Circle connections with fellow human beings. Even the religious hermit in a cave is seeking Second Circle with the divine.

We need to be known by somebody fully on every level; but like the baby in the night, many of us call out in Second Circle and remain unanswered. We need strong Second Circle connections with a partner if we are to bring children into the world, as children are going to feel more loved and secure if the adults around them are in harmony and mostly connected. Even a few decades ago, most children were brought up by a group of devoted elders that extended into the community around them. It is a very hard task to bring a child up alone.

Relationships

It seems that the more people we brush up against, the lonelier we become. A lot of dating now takes place in environments that make being in Second Circle almost impossible. How can you be present with each other in noisy bars, clubs, and restaurants if these places can only be fully negotiated in Third Circle? What's more, they are designed to encourage consumption of large amounts of alcohol and therefore create superficial meetings. These venues are great for fun and a certain Third Circle release, but not for intimacy and meeting a long-term partner.

If you are seeking intimacy, you must explore different venues that are quiet and without distractions or too much alcohol. Try to meet each other alone. Many friends go out in groups or foursomes. This can hide the fact that you and your date are not able to make Second Circle contact. My grandmother's courting always took place on walks, as her boyfriends had no money for drinks or meals. Actually, a walk in a park or the country-side encourages a couple to engage more fully with each other, although this may be best left until you are comfortable so isolated in the other person's company.

Perhaps the recent success of online matches or dating is because it gives two people a chance to communicate in a written Second Circle, which is far better than a spoken Third Circle.

With a new date, be aware that you may both be nervous and that this can throw someone into a shy First or a too flamboyant Third, so give each other a chance. Stay in Second and see if they respond. Keep breathing, and use an open voice. Ask direct questions. Be interested in them and see if they show the same interest in you. Maybe you remember dates when, after parting at the end of the evening, you had that dull thud of realization that you hadn't spoken about yourself all evening. Your date wasn't interested in you at all.

So, it is important to notice whether your date can sustain Second Circle with you. If not, where do they go? Are they in First or Third Circle? If you find it difficult at first to speak in Second, at least listen in Second.

As the relationship develops, actively notice whether they stay longer in Second Circle with you, which is a positive presence. A negative sign is if they begin to disconnect more often and then want to meet in venues that stop Second Circle. You might have to face the fact that they want your company but not your presence. Early signs are using a cell phone more often in your company, arriving late for dates, or always having somewhere to go after meeting you or after sex.

Second Circle Dating Questions

More complex discoveries will be revealed by the following questions:

Are they only comfortable in Second Circle physically or intellectually, but unable to connect to you emotionally?

Do they show Second Circle toward you in front of their friends and family?

Are they more present with their friends than they are with you? In other words, are you a by-product of their life? If this continues, you and the relationship are in trouble. Either they are not proud of you or they don't appreciate or like your presence.

Can they admit when they are wrong in Second Circle, and can you disagree with each other without retreating into First or attacking in Third? It is a sure sign of adult, mature, and equal respect for two people who care about each other to be able to disagree without rancor. This is only possible in Second Circle. However, if the disagreement challenges your or your partner's moral codes and one or both parties cannot shift or tolerate a difference, then the relationship will fragment from Second Circle.

When your partner disconnects from you, can you get them back into Second Circle?

Do you kiss and have sex in Second Circle with both of you fully present?

When you hold hands, does your partner pull you toward them?

Does a partner control how the contact is made or is the contact equal? Is only one partner allowed to initiate sex?

Does a partner detach from Second Circle after orgasm without any concern for the other's own sexual needs?

You can ask the same questions if you dance together. Do
they touch you with a patronizing pat or stroke you into
them?

Does a partner touch lovingly to take into account the
wholeness of you? First and Third Circle sex can be great
but not intimate. A clear and often disastrous example of
not having Second Circle sex is one of you calling out the
wrong name or forgetting your name altogether!

Is there only Second Circle contact between you when you
or they are being mean and spiteful, or laughing at each
other?

Is charm between you conducted in Third Circle?

Answering these questions will clearly tell you the state of a
relationship. Even if the answers paint a negative picture, you
can still try to salvage it by working to be in Second Circle with
a positive and loving energy. If you don't take action, the relationship will stifle one or both of you.

Any relationship not conducted positively in Second Circle
is doomed. And if you pretend you are in Second Circle with a
lover or spouse when you know you don't have real care and
connection with them, you will be very unhappy. The relationship is unequal; worse, there is nothing to build on as the foun-
dations are not present. Soulmates do enjoy full Second Circle
connection and an intimate relationship through the body,
heart, mind, and spirit.

Of course, the remarks above apply only to those seeking equal relationships. Some people—whether consciously or
subconsciously—will seek out the destruction of unequal and
often abusive partners so that they don't have to live in Second
Circle.

Love is, above all else, the gift of oneself.   —JEAN ANOUILH

Marriage

> If you would marry suitably, marry your equal.   —Ovid

If you are lucky enough to marry a soulmate, you still have to work at staying present with each other. Stress, children, long working hours, money worries, friends, and parents-in-law can easily knock you out of connection with each other, whether physically or emotionally, intellectually or spiritually. In marriage you must try to establish a daily practice to reconnect some part of you. This could be a moment together before you go to bed or an intimate, caring phone call.

You should try to sustain a real Second Circle interest in each other's life and well-being. Go out together without other people around you. Enjoy each other's ideas and passions. Talk about your histories together, and if you accompany your partner to an event that interests them, go willingly in Second Circle. Please try not to sulk in First or get aggressive in Third if you attend your partner's work party or their long-awaited visit to the theatre. It is better not to go at all if you can't attend positively in Second Circle. Keep the equality in place and the channels open—give and take in Second Circle. Be honest about your problems and fears together. As a couple you should try to meet in Second Circle, even if you each also have time and space alone. Many successful partners can have long periods away from each other but return to a real relationship in Second after venturing into new worlds on their own.

Sex

> And those who come together in the night and are entwined
> in rocking delight do an earnest work and gather sweetnesses,
> gather depth and strength for the song of some coming poet,
> who will arise to speak of ecstasies beyond telling.
>   —Rainer Maria Rilke, *Letters to a Young Poet*

Here is the advice given to a friend when he was seventeen by an older and more experienced mistress: "Just give me your full and absolute attention from the first look, touch, kiss . . . and you will be a great lover." Women, imagine how great sex would be if all fathers gave their sons the same advice! This advice is describing clear Second Circle energy from your lover. And men, you must know that most women need an intimate connection in order to trust you enough to really enjoy sex.

The advice given to young Englishwomen in Victorian times was intended to actively stop them connecting to their husbands, with no opportunity to enjoy sex. Mothers supposedly told daughters, on their wedding night, to "lie back and think of England." This may well have encouraged a Second Circle focus—but on an Empire, not the husband!

It was expected that a good wife would remain in First Circle, under the domination of a Third Circle husband. It was a shock to me when I learned that, apparently, in Victorian times up to one in four privately owned houses in London were brothels. This shows just how few marriages existed in Second.

There are still cultures that believe women shouldn't enjoy sex. It is another sobering fact that the brilliant New Zealand writer Katherine Mansfield was certified and placed in an asylum by her parents in the early twentieth century for masturbation, and that a young girl was circumcised in the United States as late as the 1950s when her parents found her masturbating.

So, intimate, fully present sex starts with Second Circle contact with the intended partner. Don't rush this. Be in the moment—and let the moments take as long as you both need. Make full Second Circle eye contact, extend that to touch, and then breathe to each other.

In equal lovemaking you can free yourself from the necessity of always having huge orgasms. The Second Circle will manifest great orgasms, but only if you put the real importance on physical intimacy. And remember to stay in Second Circle with each other after sex.

If you have already consummated what feels like an important relationship, go back and start again. Play a game of going on a date for the first time—look, touch, kiss, and make love in a very conscious Second Circle. If you care about each other, you will feel more free to call back your partner if you sense they are drifting out of Second Circle.

27

Communities

Communities are especially important today because they are breaking down at a time when many of us have no immediate family.

Here is a heartwarming story to start this section on community. It is the tale of "Androcles and the Lion," which George Bernard Shaw used as the basis for his play.

Androcles, an early Christian in the Roman Empire, met a lion on a woodland path. The lion was in tremendous pain from a thorn in his paw. Androcles removed the thorn and they parted friends. Fast forward to Androcles in the Roman Coliseum, about to face the lions. The lion, of course, recognized Androcles, and instead of eating him they embraced and waltzed together.

The relevance of this story is simple. The more you help people in and around your community, the greater the chance that they will one day give back. The giving is an act of positive presence fundamental to survival. One of the reasons that the human species is, anthropologically speaking, so successful on the planet is our strong ability to create communities.

A group of humans crossing the Kalahari Desert need each other. Together, they can chase off lions, search for food, hunt and share the meat, look after the children, and carry the old. Any member who doesn't stay present to the group and lives off the community without giving back will be left behind, to be eaten by the lions. The example is closer to us than we think. In order to survive, we need each other, and that need can only be fully expressed if we are present together—be it in our communities or in successful work teams. This presence humanizes our joint endeavors to survive and enhances a good, meaningful life.

The more people in your immediate community who know you in Second Circle, the safer you and your family will be. There can be no community until we are present with each other, and without community we are in danger of losing this essential connection, built deeply into our DNA, with our own species.

Start by marking your territory with positive presence. This doesn't mean cultivating deep friendships with people around you, but it does mean making regular Second Circle contact. This might include the exchange of names, basic opinions about the day, the weather, or the state of the world, enquiring about the family, holidays, or sharing a funny story. As long as this is an equal exchange and not competitive, the day will be richer for you both. A major joy of dog ownership is being able to build up community through the act of dog walking.

Simple acts of caring and acknowledging each other are a good place to start. These exchanges could be with, among others, any of the following:

Neighbors
Newspaper vendors
Garage attendants
Street cleaners
Gardeners
Salespeople
Waiters

Even eye contact and a nod or a wave, a "How are you?", the opening of a door for someone, or any recognition of another's presence, all done and received in Second Circle, humanizes your own world as much as someone else's.

Check on neighbors and notice when you haven't seen them for a while. I know that I felt much safer at night around the National Theatre knowing most of the beggars by name, and there have been occasions when they have looked out for me.

In smaller communities this behavior is more natural, although even these are being destroyed by the automobile, as people are not walking and therefore not meeting. It requires real work in larger urban living, but it is the only way to live richly and safely.

If you want to know your home and its surroundings, then be present in your community. I was working in Athens during the 1990s when a terrible murder case was reported in England. Two young boys (both age ten) abducted a two-year-old child from a shopping mall near Liverpool, then walked the toddler over two miles before killing him. Now, you know how hard it is walking a toddler, particularly if they are unhappy. There must have been some sort of struggle to walk him that distance. What my Athenian friends couldn't comprehend was why no one on that journey knew at least one of the boys abducting the toddler, or knew the toddler. Several people noticed the distressed child and questioned the older boys, but then simply accepted their explanation that he was lost and they were taking him to the police station. This appalling crime unfolded because there was no community; no one knew the boys. I don't believe it is because we don't care for each other that these care-less crimes happen. I think it is because we don't know each other enough to dare to care.

28

Education

No man can reveal to you aught but that which already lies half asleep in the dawning of our own knowledge. . . .

If [the teacher] is indeed wise he does not bid you enter the house of wisdom, but rather leads you to the threshold of your own mind.

—Khalil Gibran, *The Prophet*

This section is for anyone who teaches or learns. That could be in schools, colleges, universities, or when information is shared among colleagues in the workplace. By now you might know that deep, active, and thorough learning only takes place when teacher and student are both in Second Circle. It will also help if the teacher is passionate about the subject as it is very hard for a student to stay interested without a teacher's full involvement.

Third Circle teaching, which is an occupational hazard, might control the students and impart surface learning, but that learning is passive and generally shallow. Even when students try to learn in Second, they have to employ enormous amounts of willpower to stay in Second with a Third Circle teacher. I have no desire to blame teachers for adopting Third Circle energy as it seems the most immediate way of engaging a group of threatening students. It is, after all, a good defense strategy.

In fairness to teachers, most of them have no voice training. In Britain, such training disappeared from teacher training in the late 1970s, as a cost-cutting exercise. As a costly result, not only do teachers suffer vocal exhaustion and regularly lose their voices, but they can hardly impart education if they can't be heard or are only audible by shouting. We all know that no one listens accurately to a shouter, and being taught in Third only encourages a sulking First or a confronting Third in the student.

A First Circle teacher has no chance of teaching anything unless he or she is a renowned guru, whose students have flocked to hear every word and are willing to move into the teacher's First Circle by actually bowing forward to hear the words.

Vast numbers of teachers try to—and long to—do a great job. This is hard if they are under so many pressures, demands, and restrictions placed on them by society and government. Only the most highly skilled teachers can remain present and fully effective under such strain. Many really care but are attacked if they don't seem to be solving all the problems of an unpresent society.

> What nobler employment, or more valuable to the state, than that of the man who instructs the rising generation.
>
> —Cicero

Great teaching takes place in the moment, but it is very hard to be present if you are being told what and how to teach. Teachers struggle to fulfill government directives and place their schools high on test tables, and the easiest way to get good test results is teaching by rote, which can be easily achieved in Third Circle. I know that tests have their place in education; but if a teacher and student cannot be creative and divert from a narrow route that merely answers a specific question, they will never experience excellence, or stay curious and caring about their subject. Teaching-by-the-numbers might have short-term results, but it doesn't educate deeply, individually, or for the future.

If students are unable to be in Second Circle because their family hasn't been present with them, they are at a huge disadvantage. It lands heavily and unfairly on the teacher to train such students to be present before they can begin to educate them.

You see this lack of presence in children who have been neglected at home, but you also see it in children who have such ambitious and competitive parents that the child finds it easier to be in First or Third as a direct response. Both the neglected and the driven child can revolt by detachment or a "fuck you" aggression.

Here are two stories from my very early teaching days about two teachers who taught me how to respect the rights of the child and student.

I did a long student teaching stint in an inner-city school. Most of the children lived in projects and came from fragmented families.

The class teacher I was assisting was a woman in her sixties. In the staffroom she was treated as a bit of a joke, and I had the distinct feeling the principal couldn't wait for her retirement. With the rest of the staff she was shy—she knew she was under threat and was very aware that the principal hated the way she taught as she didn't stick to the curriculum. But she was a brilliant teacher.

I will never forget the gifts of love, wisdom, and healing she gave to those deprived children. They loved her, felt safe, and performed unexaminable tasks well above their age ability.

Picture a typical Monday morning in winter. These five-year-old kids had been shut up all weekend watching TV and would come into the open-plan space stir-crazy. She would allow the chaos for a bit. She never raised her voice but would sit still watching their release, remaining present, loving, and concerned. Within minutes they would gather quietly around her, breathe with her, and she could begin to teach gently and clearly.

She stayed present with one girl who was so disturbed that she was covering the toilet walls with her own excrement. The teacher wasn't shocked but cleaned the walls with the girl, talking all the time to her in Second Circle. She gave the girl tidying tasks and responsibilities, and there was no more excrement on the toilet walls.

She was the person who noticed that a boy had been wearing the same set of filthy clothes for days and took action. She found out that his mother had left him alone for a week.

She stood by me when I suggested that the naughtiest child in the class was partially deaf and the principal was disparaging my idea. The child proved to have little hearing and had taught herself to lip-read, speak, and read—how clever is that!

This teacher never had discipline problems, unlike the rest of the staff, and she never spoke negatively about a child.

So, what was her secret? Before any knowledge was imparted or class started, she and the children sat together, still and present. She would make clear eye contact with each child, and when they were present the work began. She didn't care if this took time and she taught what she sensed they could learn. So, sometimes it was math instead of reading. And sometimes there was a story before writing. Her timetable was out of order, but her teaching wasn't, and through disorder the children learned order.

Today, that remarkable woman would not be allowed to teach, but I know she is gold in the bones and memories of her pupils. There are middle-aged men and women in London as I write this who are only surviving because of her and are probably better parents because of her love and faith in them as five-year-olds.

My second story is one of intrusion. When teachers are in Second Circle they know when it is the right moment to teach, and if the subject requires touch, then they know when and how to touch.

Many years ago an eighty-year-old acting coach said to me, "I never touch anyone if there is any agenda in my touch. It's taken me forty years to know that."

Now this was in the 1970s, when it was cool to touch! I have thought about this nearly every day since hearing it. The simplicity and truth of this remark will always remain with me. To touch effectively you have to be in Second Circle, but if there is an agenda the student will always feel it.

Equally, whatever you say has to have no agenda except the well-being and growth of the student, and this can only be gauged in Second Circle. As a teacher you must speak the truth when the student can receive it in Second Circle. It might hurt, but it is not cruel if there is no agenda, no desire, no spite, no revenge, no dislike . . . only the student's enlightenment.

If you are a teacher you must work on Second Circle through your body, breath, and voice, as this direct communication is a huge part of your chosen profession. Not only will you be more effective as a teacher but you will have a healthier voice on Friday afternoons. Believe it or not, there is a vocal syndrome called "Friday Afternoon Voice" which is very common among teachers, who have such strained voices that they can't speak over the weekend. This is a sure sign of Third Circle teaching.

Challenging the Teacher

If you teach in Second Circle, you can feel and anticipate a challenging student. In First or Third Circle, these challenges are more likely to take you by surprise.

Intelligent and very talented students are often the ones who challenge and it is sometimes a compliment to your teaching that they feel free enough to do so. A good, healthy challenge comes in Second Circle; but most come in Third Circle or as a muttered remark in First Circle, which you are not supposed to hear. Using your positive presence, draw the Third Circle challenge into Second, and ask calmly for the First Circle one to repeat what they have said.

A good response is to engage with the challenge, stay open, perhaps even admitting that you don't know the answer! See the student's point of view, put it in context, and offer to explore the ideas behind the challenge—if not at that moment, which might disturb the lesson's form, then at a more appropriate time.

This approach makes the whole class feel safe and defuses any aggression they might feel for you or your subject. The challenge can be educational for you as well as for the students. Any challenge in life can be accepted if the challenge is made appropriately, and the teacher by responding with grace teaches the challenger to eventually challenge with grace. This is a skill that can make our life easier in all contexts—a skill that can get you promoted and even loved.

I hope I do teach in this way, but I certainly have given the worst possible responses in the past. That is, going into a very energized Third Circle to prove a student wrong, giving example after example of why I am right. I have even gone home and rifled through textbooks to prove them wrong. This will make the student either withdraw from you or pledge to catch you out on every mistake you make. Either way, learning is impaired. The less secure members of the class will disappear further into themselves and you will be controlling through Third Circle fear.

29

The Workplace

Most of us have to work. It takes up a huge portion of our lives, and my generation—those born in the decades after World War II—will probably have to work until we are seventy. Many feel that they have no choice in their careers, which is often untrue, and even those with choice can get stuck and spend years losing the will to live.

I have to ask the question that will affect your whole life and well-being, a question you can ask at any point in your life: Do you want success in your work?

If the answer is yes, then you will need to be in Second Circle to achieve your success. In Second Circle you will feel passionate enough in your heart and mind to fuel that success. Of course, you can manage some progress and success through Third Circle, but to move into responsible power you have to shift from Third into Second. If you don't, you will lose the joy and passion in your work and have no respect or community around you.

Notice how middle management is full of Third Circle bluffers who rarely get promoted and operate with cynicism and a sense of defeat. Success also requires hard work, and you never get sustainable success if you are lazy. The work and commitment required for Second Circle throughout your body, mind, and heart is the antithesis of laziness. If you are lazy, you are not in Second Circle. Laziness is expressed in either a detached First Circle or a bluffed Third as you try to prove to the world that you are working.

If the answer to my question about success is no, you don't want power and success, it is completely justifiable to make that decision. Not everyone wants the stress and struggle that success requires. This brings me to a second question: Do you want to have a fulfilling work life, even if it doesn't involve promotion?

I believe an honest reply would be yes; but if you don't stay in Second, you will slip into a detached First and spend most of your life absent from yourself and others in order to earn money. This is not entirely your full responsibility as many workplaces actively encourage detachment. You mustn't succumb to this tyranny—you should seek work that will enable you to be present.

The introduction of the assembly line in Henry Ford's factory had a lot to do with a mass of workers becoming the sleeping masses. An assembly line can only keep flowing if the workers don't care about the product or have a passion for it. Ford didn't want craftsmen in the assembly process. A craftsman cares about his work, and care keeps you in Second with any task you perform. If you had cared on a Ford assembly line, you would have stopped the line if you saw a dent in a hubcap, and Henry would have lost productivity and millions of dollars.

> Technology . . . the knack of so arranging the world that we
> need not experience it.   —MAX FRISCH

Seeking Success

Don't be beguiled or choose a role model for success by imitating those in Third Circle who are pushing themselves to the top—

they rarely get there. This is particularly important for women to understand: the workplace is depressingly full of ambitious women adopting the worst habits of men in the guise of Third Circle, and consequently losing their female skills of Second Circle intimacy.

Begin to realize that when you are not in Second Circle, events will pass you by and those with power over you will notice either your absence (First) or your generalized challenge to them (Third).

Action for Success

- Notice your bosses. Are they in Second or Third? If they are in First, they are not doing their job and probably need others around them plastering the cracks. You might have to make a choice as to whether you want to continually save them from their own apathy.
- Stay in Second at every important meeting. Even when those around you are bored and drifting off into First, your presence will be noticed.
- Staying in Second at work reveals whether there are gaps in your skills and whether you need training in different skills to succeed. In Second it will be apparent whether you can and will move up the organization. You will know whether the organization wants your positive presence or whether it challenges employees and makes everyone around you uneasy. Some organizations don't want success; the company gets by and is threatened by a dynamic force.

  With Second Circle attention, you will be aware of all the obstacles blocking your pathway to promotion.
- Don't be drawn into apathy by First Circlers' bluff or by those who operate in Third.

When you reach your goal, you have to stay more in Second Circle as you can never relax with power. Indeed, you will have to be more present as others will seek your position.

Action for Job Satisfaction

- Work in a company where at least part of the work engages your passion and interest.
- If that is not possible, you might have to consider some form of retraining, and actively seek out knowledge that will enable you to work in a company that allows your passion and care to thrive.
- If you find yourself for any period of your life in a dead-end job, at least make some attempts to have Second Circle connections around you. Find shared interests with your colleagues. Do your best at the job as this will instill some positive presence in the workplace.

Muhammad Ali made an advertisement some years ago saying he would have been the best at anything he did, even if he was a garbage collector.

A good piece of work requires Second Circle attention to detail. Even a carefully prepared sandwich is an act of positive Second Circle presence.

Dead-End Jobs

There are many forms of dead-end job, but the worst of them tend to be done by people trapped in poverty and debt, with the inability to access an education that would be a road out of their situation. However, even those stuck in seemingly dead-end jobs can be deeply appreciated when they produce a great cup of coffee made with Second Circle care. Strong Second Circle bonds formed on the factory floor can transform lives.

Occasionally, remarkable spirits fight their way out. I've had students, all amazing, who through raw determination and intelligence have crawled out of these traps. These are some of the most inspirational people on the planet, but they are rare, and the fate of the uneducated can be bleak.

I remember overhearing a comment made at a retirement party in a grotty South London pub: "I've worked thirty-seven years for that f****** company and all they've given me is a box of chocolates!" How tragic that a person's entire working life could end in such a demoralizing way.

My own epiphany was working in a library when I was eighteen and observing the despair of the older staff, who felt lost in their work. Many had dreamed of being writers or performers but had chosen security over their passion and not knowing over failure. Some spent their whole day plotting minor adventures to escape, which could include hiding in the toilet for hours on end. One said to me, "I like books; the problem with this job is the people."

Furthermore, a job might pay you well and give you security, but there are no challenges in the areas that can feed your life and presence. These are successful jobs, yet they can be emotionally and spiritually dead.

Not long ago I heard a young man say to his friend, "I got an excellent degree in science and I'm making a lot of money in a huge company, but actually I'm working on producing better toilet rolls." He sounded so disappointed; but at least his education meant that he could, with a little Second Circle motivation, make a change. The lucky ones are the people who have choice.

Whenever I work in the corporate world, I see that such work challenges many to rethink their lives and the way they operate. One young man, twenty-five and earning $400,000 a year, recalled in one of our exercises how alive he felt on safari. Seeing the power of a leopard in a tree above his head, he made Second Circle eye contact with it. Two years later, he wrote to tell me he had given up his huge salary and was now working in conservation.

30

The Corporate World

Power consists in one's capacity to link his will with the purpose of others, to lead by reason and a gift of cooperation.

—WOODROW WILSON, Letter to Mary A. Hulbert

A little touch of Harry in the night.

—WILLIAM SHAKESPEARE, *Henry V*

All great leaders have charisma, love, and passion for their work and operate in Second. The presence and openness of a leader filters down through a company and is an appropriate encouragement to everyone to work in Second Circle.

The encouragement of Second Circle means employees work hard for them, feel appreciated, recognized, and are loyal. They feel in some ways equal to their leader and are able to challenge them and contribute as a band of brothers.

CEOs who communicate in First or Third do not instill trust, loyalty, or passion among their employees. In this scenario the company may suffer, and change and growth may become impaired because the leader is effectively blocking the creative energy of the company's richest resource: human intelligence and passion.

Great military leaders know that if you have to ask your troops to follow you without question, you have more chance if you address them personally, equally, and intimately. A Third Circle rallying address might be impressive, magnificent, and effective, but it is hard to remember when the gruesome business of war begins. In the darkest days of World War II, Winston Churchill spoke absolutely in Second Circle to the British people and included himself in the war: "I have nothing to offer but blood, toil, tears and sweat." And again:

> We shall defend our island, whatever the cost may be, we shall fight on the beaches, we shall fight on the landing grounds, we shall fight in the fields and in the streets, we shall fight in the hills; we shall never surrender.

He became equal with his people. The "we" put him right in the heart of the struggle.

Shakespeare explores the same connection between Henry V and his troops before the Battle of Agincourt. This beleaguered king connects with his men in Second Circle. With this real bond, a vastly outnumbered army defeats its enemy.

> We few, we happy few, we band of brothers.
> For he to-day that sheds his blood with me
> Shall be my brother.

A First Circle CEO is likely to depress the workforce, and a Third Circle one might mentally motivate with a generalized energy but rarely produces an open and creative atmosphere. At worst, a Third Circle CEO can intimidate the workforce.

Leaders in Third Circle don't like challenge. They can humiliate, ignore, shout down, and mock their employees into submission. They don't listen, and a wrongly timed Second Circle challenge can have you segregated out of the group, sidelined, and even fired. The rest of the employees become bystanders who are complicit in the bullying of a colleague and who live in fear.

As a member of a company, you get noticed and can rapidly succeed when you are present and actively seeking excellence. Be present in one-to-one encounters and in meetings, however large, as your Second Circle energy will illuminate and shine in the usual First Circle energy of large workforces.

You might have to negotiate your Second Circle and use it with care if your immediate boss is in either First or Third and feels threatened. If a company doesn't want your power and presence, you will have to relocate for fulfillment and success.

Begin to recognize if you are good at Second Circle in one-to-one but not in large groups. This is often the case with women. Or perhaps your strength is Second Circle with a group, but you are unable to do this one-to-one. Generally, more men fall into this category. As you realize your strengths, you must work to stay in Second in the area of your weakness.

It is completely true that companies function better and are more productive, with happier employees, when Second Circle contact is encouraged. This challenges the old style of management, command and control, which can be threatened by a present and alert workforce. Third Circle control is used by old-order thinkers. If you find yourself in this type of company, you can begin to humanize those around you through Second Circle contact. Receptionists, cleaners, colleagues, and even your most immediate boss will be grateful. After a while, you will notice a shift in the positive energy of your environment.

As you tune up to Second Circle in yourself and others, you will identify the culture of energy in every building you enter—the energy that comes from the top and seeps down to the very basement of the building.

At job interviews, you will be able to sense whether you are entering a Second Circle friendly space. Doing business with other organizations, you will rapidly recognize their culture and know sooner whether the ride will be pleasant or not. Healthy companies are present and open. They are the companies that provide present and caring services to their public.

In the last decade or so there has been a shift toward some powerful companies, such as banks, supermarkets, and credit card companies, treating their customers and providers in a dismissive, often cynical Third Circle way.

> A banker is a fellow who lends you his umbrella when the sun is shining, but wants it back the minute it begins to rain.
>
> —MARK TWAIN

> I believe that banking institutions are more dangerous to our liberties than standing armies. If the American people ever allow private banks to control the issue of their currency, first by inflation then by deflation, the banks and corporations that will grow up around [the banks] will deprive the people of all property until their children wake up homeless on the continent their fathers conquered. The issuing power should be taken from the banks and restored to the people, to whom it properly belongs.
>
> —THOMAS JEFFERSON, Letter to Secretary of the Treasury Albert Gallatin, 1802

It used to be possible to be treated as a human being and to receive Second Circle attention from your bank manager, but this is now rare, although it is your money. We have all felt powerless as we try to get some Second Circle contact and understanding from telephone call centers. It is the equivalent of being lost in a Third Circle maze—and what a relief if you encounter a concerned voice within that maze.

Most supermarkets treat their employees, suppliers, the farmers who work the land to make a living, and their customers with Third Circle disdain. This is extraordinary as it dehumanizes the very people who keep these stores open. We sometimes, as consumers, understand the full contempt some of the multinationals feel for us—the sleeping masses.

Supposedly, the chairman of a leading credit card company was heard to joke that his customers were idiots for paying such high interest rates. And the owner of a chain of jewelers once said that his merchandise was "rubbish"—he wouldn't buy it. That remark lost him his company. A confidence trickster cannot think of his victim in Second Circle; they musn't be human. We need to be dehumanized, perceived as fools who deserve to be tricked.

Autolycus, Shakespeare's confidence trickster, remarks in *The Winter's Tale*, "What a fool honesty is." This jovial trickster laughs at those who believe him, are kind to him as he steals from them.

Truth and honesty only exist if you have a Second Circle dialogue with yourself and specific people in the world.

> The problem of power is how to achieve its responsible use rather than its irresponsible one—and how to get men of power to live for the public rather than off the public.
>
> —ROBERT F. KENNEDY

The corporate world should invest in Second Circle behavior within its own walls and outside them. In the long term, the company's life would be healthier, more prosperous, and honest as a result.

> Pleasure in the job puts perfection in the work.
>
> —ARISTOTLE

To finish this chapter, I am going to explore the activities that are essential if you are to be successful. There are many others I could describe, but these are the topics that come up regularly and concern many people I deal with in workshops. Actually, you can transfer these skills to a number of other important events in your work and personal life.

Closing a Deal

Every great salesperson sells in Second Circle. If they lose their confidence and flounder into First or Third during a sale, the deal can fail.

Just listen to a good phone sales pitch. You can't get off the phone politely if the salesperson stays in Second. You can only escape when you hear them shift into First or Third. A good salesperson can stay in Second even if they are masking their presence in First or Third. You can notice how they seem to be in First while you read the fine print of an agreement or when they pick up a phone to another client but are still with you.

To close a deal, stay in Second, even if you have to withdraw at certain stages of the negotiations into a seeming First Circle. Third Circle is to be avoided as it is unattractive. Use your deep Second Circle breath and breathe to your client. Sit in a chair that allows you to keep your back straight and set your feet on the floor. It is useful if you can push gently with one hand against an armrest or desk to engage the breath. This intensifies Second Circle if you feel the deal is floundering.

Enter any room and start negotiations in Second Circle. Even the seemingly casual chat before negotiations begin will focus you and your client. As you shake hands, stay constantly in Second. There is nothing casual about important business and importance is always expressed in Second Circle.

Remember to finish in Second; don't wander off into First or Third, even when the deal is done. Staying in Second makes a stronger impression and is mannerly and gracious.

Save your best selling points for the moments when the client is in Second and fully listening to you. In a clear Second, you will draw them out if they are in First and break through their shell if they are in Third. Even if you don't make the deal, stay in Second, as this will keep your connection and shows your resilience.

If you employ these strategies, you will be a great salesperson. By that I mean you will sell to people who get to know you a little, and that can mean that you won't want to bulldoze them into a deal they don't really want. Second Circle selling is possibly more ethical, so you may lose a few deals, but you will gain long-term trust in the clients who do buy from you.

Interviews or Presentations

You really do have the optimum chance of success if you are interviewed or make a presentation in Second Circle.

Many of those you are interviewed by and present to are keen to knock you off your pedestal. They may deliberately adopt a front that is offputting and encourages you to pull yourself up into Third Circle or give up into First Circle. A panel in First can depress you. A Third Circle panel can make you aggressive. As can audiences receiving your presentation.

Please fight these temptations, as you might be all right in an interview or presentation in Third, but you won't be great. In First Circle you haven't a hope in hell! Both interviews and presentations are formal occasions and should never be attempted in First. If any event is important, it deserves Second Circle energy. If you are aggressively questioned or heckled, stay in Second.

Remember, if you fail an interview and have been in Second Circle, at least you know they saw you and you did your best. If you succeed in Third, they might be getting someone they really don't want and you might find yourself in an unsuitable job.

Preparation

- Before entering a room, get into Second Circle body and breathe in deeply, silently, and calmly. If there is a wall you can push against without others seeing you, push and breathe. If you feel sluggish, walk up and down with energy. Release your shoulders.

- As you enter the room, breathe it in Second.
- Make eye contact with the panel and definitely do so as you shake hands in Second Circle.
- Start when you are ready and on the breath. Don't rush yourself out of Second Circle.
- Listen in Second. If asked questions, don't interrupt until the person has finished. Rushing will place you in First; bluffing into Third.
- Be clear and direct, with an open voice.
- Stay curious and gracious.

31

Professions Reliant on Second Circle

There are certain professions and vocations that can only be successfully performed in Second Circle energy. However, that energy might only be in part of you—your body or your mind. You will be richer in yourself and your life, though, if you can operate completely in Second Circle.

Sports

Great winners in sport are in Second Circle. There are flukes when a shot scores accidentally without the intention of Second Circle; but one of the reasons people flock to watch great sporting performances is that we are watching presence and its life-giving force.

Amateur players can often bluff their way in Third, but this generalized aggression or enthusiasm is messy and can lead to blunders which end up being used in comedy routines or joked about after the game. You can watch video outtakes on TV and see countless Third Circle sporting attempts failing magnificently. The generalized, eager kick that has the kicker landing on his back; the earnest diver, showing off and not fully focusing, her belly flopping in a spectacular Third Circle splash.

A First Circle team member is a liability to the team, and at school those First Circle energy players are the last to be chosen as their vacancy inevitably creates a vacuum on the sports field.

Many of us engage in sports, sometimes extreme ones, in order to find Second Circle engagement, to feel alive and vivid. These sports relieve mundane lives, and after playing there is a buzz and passion that seeps into life.

Performance

Great performers are in Second Circle, and their ability to stay focused in Second Circle can be the difference between the mediocre actor and the good to great one.

It is possible to be a fine musician and play in First or Third. Some modern dancers seem to make a career in First, as do some nightclub singers, but their work fades rapidly in our memory. It is hard to remember the dance or the song the next day.

Performers must know that audiences are yearning to be brought back into their Second Circle through their work. The reason we spend money on concerts and theatre is to be shocked back into presence. You can enjoy a show that is in Third, but you are not transformed by it. The clue to performance is in the word "live." We are seeking life from live performance and life is the energy of Second Circle. We are transformed by performers in Second Circle as long as we too are in Second. When this happens, we remember performances decades after experiencing them.

There has been an unfortunate trend recently in the theatre for productions to excite an audience with a great deal of Third Circle energy. The audience is swamped in unspecific energy and believes it is having a great experience as it is whipped up into Third. These shows are effective, but not humane. You don't care about characters or their stories even though you enjoy the surrounding effects.

To some extent, production values create this problem. Massive sets, projections, and amplified music can all reduce the performer to a cog on a machinelike stage that has lost its human space and individuality. Naturally, the performer's response in being surrounded by Third Circle energy is to push up into Third to compete.

There are also issues of performance space design. If the space is too disconnected from the human body's proportion, then Second Circle energy from the performer and from the audience is harder to achieve. Most venues for rock stars are pure Third Circle—part of the buzz for the audience is to lose themselves and join a crowd in Third Circle. However, when a great Second Circle performer hones this energy, then the audience can be transformed into Second. When I saw the Beatles in their early days, I was among a mass of screaming girls and the band members were tiny dots on the stage, but I could see John Lennon clearly. His Second Circle was so strong.

If seats are too comfortable in theatres or concert halls, the audience has a harder time to stay present. They may fall into a comfortable First or spread into Third. Some directors even advocate harder seats to keep the audience alert in Second Circle.

The Arts

Great writers write in Second Circle and their work will change and move you if you read it in Second Circle. You might only respond to a great novel in a rereading. That could be because you read it initially in First or Third. This is easy to do if a book intimidates you—you fear that you will not understand it—but you won't deeply understand anything if you don't read in Second Circle.

Anything written in First or Third is not good! It can be effective, but the writer's lack of presence makes it seem trivial, sentimental, or at worst reduces our connection with humanity.

Try this experiment: Read a tabloid article or a blockbuster novel designed as a quick airport or holiday read in Second Circle. You will be shocked by the quality of writing or bored by the content. This type of material can help to zone you out or wind you down from too much unspecific presence, but as daily fodder it will destroy your verbal sensibility and imagination.

Try the same experiment with mass-market movies and TV shows. In Second, you realize that they are designed to be watched in First or Third. Conversely, by watching TV and movies in Second Circle, you will again discover the quality material and meet the great actors, presenters, and writers equally.

Great documentary filmmakers want us in Second Circle and use Second Circle techniques to engage us. There is no point in exploring any truth unless you can draw your audience into Second Circle. However, directors of some blockbusters want us in Third Circle. If we watched the blowing up of people in Second Circle, it is likely we would care too much about the appalling violence and lack of humanity within the movie and walk out.

All background music is designed to be in First Circle, which is why it can drive you mad if you start to listen to it in Second Circle.

Many popular songs are written in Third Circle, although they could be sung in Second. When you catch the lyrics or tune in fully in Second Circle, you may realize that a popular song, once effective in Third, is dull in Second. Great music is written in Second and deepens you—if you listen to it in Second.

Although many of the greatest artists are in Second Circle, they might not be appreciated in their lifetime—particularly if audiences do not want to be present to a message or form that the artist is communicating. Third Circle creators can be very famous, wealthy, and successful, but don't generally last or survive the test of time. They are sometimes successful because they make an audience feel safe and detached. They can be amusing, risqué, and mocking, but not profound. Their message is relevant to a particular culture and moment in time. But without Second Circle humanity, it will not find a home in the hearts of future audiences.

If you work in a profession where you are dealing with fellow human beings under stress, if not trauma, then full human Second Circle from you is their right. However, it is these very traumas that can make many people in the professional ranks choose not to engage fully.

Some professionals have power over many of us and it is always tempting for them to feel the power rather than the humanity of their job.

The Law

Criminals. I am starting this section with the criminal. After all, we wouldn't need laws if everyone behaved well and harmoniously. The perpetrators of most violent and antisocial crimes are in Third Circle when they perform them. Many are blocked from being present to the humanity and distress of their victims by alcohol, drugs, blinding passion, or a Third Circle bravado fueled by other gang members.

Jesus Christ said, during his Crucifixion, "Father, forgive them, for they know not what they do." You can only really know what you do when you are in Second Circle. The intention of a crime is at the heart of our justice system. Do you know what you are doing and are you really aware of your actions? Manslaughter (Third). Murder (Second). Few crimes are committed in First, and if they are, it is an act of not being present enough to realize what is happening. The quest of any civilized justice system is to find out how aware the criminals are of their actions—how present are they?

In *Hamlet*, King Claudius has murdered his brother but doesn't know, fully and consciously, what he has done until he sees the crime enacted in a play. He calls for light, and a light actually enters his spirit as he becomes conscious of his crime: "O, my offense is rank, it smells to heaven." This is the moment he becomes present to his actions.

This understanding that Shakespeare explores is similar to recent legal schemes practiced with some criminals and their victims. The victim sits with the perpetrator of the crime. They talk and listen to each other. The criminal hears, and hopefully understands how his or her actions have hurt another human being. The victim is witnessed as a human by the criminal.

Both parties must be in Second Circle and recognize each other as valid human beings. When this recognition occurs, studies suggest that the criminal rarely reoffends. Meeting the victim brings the crime into sharp clarity, and the unfairness experienced by the victim affects the perpetrator.

Many crimes are committed in Second Circle, and these criminals are hardened and are less likely to thaw in the presence of their victims. The hardening of offenders can happen rapidly when they are living among more violent prison inmates. When I started teaching in prisons, I saw how hard it is to survive inside without detaching yourself from your emotions— First Circle emotional disconnection. I also saw how necessary it was to stay alert in a physical Second Circle.

Prison teaches emotional First Circle coupled with physical Second Circle. This energy cocktail is completely destructive to society as it will result in emotionally careless violence!

Working with prisoners and hearing their stories, I began to understand another energy conundrum: their first crimes and arrests were made worse by an inability to communicate clearly in Second Circle.

Here is a common scenario: a minor incident rolling out of control as the perpetrator goes into a higher state of Third Circle. Because most law enforcement officers operate in Third Circle— and you can't blame them, as Third Circle is a shield to deflect the constant abuse they suffer—you can picture the scene as two Third Circle energies clash. Neither has a chance to see the humanity or rationality of the other.

When I started teaching prisoners in my early twenties, I had had, as many young people have, brushes with the law. I had survived arrest and avoided prison because I had the knowledge and background to stay present with the policeman. You definitely have a greater chance of being given a warning if you stay present to the officer—as long as the offense is minor!

The police. A Second Circle police officer arrests in Second Circle and can identify the hardheaded crimes from the chaotic and stupid acts we all sometimes perform. When a Second Circle policeman lets you off, it is because he has recognized that you performed a stupid one-off act that will not be repeated—particularly if you are sufficiently ashamed and in Second Circle.

Fruitful interrogation is carried out in Second Circle, as an emotional Second Circle can capture the trust of a criminal and perhaps gain a confession. The intellectual Second Circle interrogator forensically understands the lies of a suspect.

A great police officer will be present to the victim's pain and therefore help to heal it and extract more details of the crime. The victim will feel important and help the police more readily as their loss has been witnessed.

Police partners in Second Circle together move as a team and protect each other. This is because intimate Second Circle bonding in the police or armed forces produces better results—you care for each other and, under stress, that is enormously empowering.

If you are stopped by the police, most officers will deal with you in Third. The worst move on your part is to meet them in Third. This energy in you could explode and appear as a challenge, accelerating the situation and potentially increasing any charges against you.

First Circle deference—the low-profile, off-voice apology—can work, but this can encourage a patronizing response, which won't allow you to shift the officer into Second Circle.

You really want to encourage any authority figure into Second Circle with you. They can then appreciate you as an equal human being and you have more chance of appeal.

Stay in Second. Make eye contact. Breathe to them. Physical touching is not a good idea! Stay open in your body. Speak to them but don't raise your voice; be reasonable, and if you disagree with anything they say, try to explain yourself in a clear, unagitated way.

The professional hazard of being a police officer is having to stomach a constant stream of Third Circle abuse and derision from the public; it will be a relief to meet with you in a calm and reasonable Second Circle.

You might not be let off the offense, but it will be a less messy event than if you had conducted it in Third.

If you are innocent, a Second Circle arrest will give you the maximum opportunity of explaining yourself.

In the courtroom. Truth and justice can only be sought and found in Second Circle. The great law enforcement judges and lawyers operate in a full Second Circle. By "full," I mean a physical, intellectual, and emotional Second. And they know how to switch off energies when required.

Any lawyer working in Second Circle will gain the trust of his or her clients. People go to lawyers when they feel wronged, and a present lawyer is often recommended ahead of a more intelligent one. Obviously, an intelligent and present one is the optimum choice, but under duress a person needs present care, particularly as the law and its language feel dehumanizing and clinical.

In the courtroom, a present lawyer will appeal to a jury more than the flashy Third Circle one or the deenergizing First Circle presentation. Witnesses reveal more when they feel their testimony is received in Second and judges stay more attentive to Second Circle lawyers.

If you watch trials, you might have noticed all of this, but I am sure you have also seen how badly the law is served by mumbling, passionless First Circle lawyers, who are often inaudible to both judge and jury. This is useless to either the prosecution or the defense.

Equally offputting is the Third Circle overpresented case that lacks present Second Circle heart. All witnesses will respond better to Second Circle cross-examination, unless they have something to hide, which will be noticed by a Second Circle lawyer.

A great judge should listen in a clear and complete Second Circle to every bit of evidence without showing boredom (First) or contempt (Third). Each jury member should aim to be listening in Second Circle. If the judge and jury are present, then the case is heard. If not, then justice can be arbitrary and at worst not seen to be done by any of the parties—the accused and the accuser. In *The Winter's Tale*, the innocent Hermione realizes that she is being tried by a corrupt legal system:

'Tis rigour, and not law.

If you are to believe in justice, then we all have to be in Second Circle in order for justice to thrive.

Politics

Great politicians win votes, hearts, and minds in Second Circle. We need to be able to believe and trust in their power and, if necessary, follow them to war. It seems to me that voters should demand that their elected leaders are Second Circle politicians, and that these politicians must engage the public in the process of government and represent them with positive presence and humanity.

Winston Churchill addressed the British in the darkest days

of World War II in Second Circle. He had to; no one would have believed a shallow rabble-rousing Third Circle or a hidden passionless First. And the British responded in Second. Both Churchill and the British needed to survive in Second Circle.

Bill Clinton was a natural Second Circle politician, and therein lay his power, a great deal of which was only lost when he lied on TV about Monica Lewinsky. Then, he moved very clearly into Third Circle.

Tony Blair had his moments, particularly when they were unscripted and unprepared. This happened when he spoke immediately after the death of Princess Diana.

George W. Bush is rarely seen in Second—only in flashes, and normally with rage and malice. It startled me that he couldn't move into Second Circle survival mode upon hearing about the attacks on 9/11.

The big question is: Do we want politicians who wish to silence us and disengage us, put us to sleep, not encourage action from us? Do we wish them to drown us with a generalized Third Circle delivery or bore us into submission with First Circle? Is it right that politicians and their parties are actively encouraged not to tell us the truth—is the truth not good for the masses? If the answer to any of these questions is yes, it would explain why so many young politicians seem distant and disconnected from us all.

It is hard to maintain your connection if you are not telling the truth, and worse, if you don't believe your public deserves the truth. Many politicians remain constantly in Third Circle. They feign charm, sometimes aggression, but rarely are they present with us. But perhaps it is not always their intention to be in that energy.

Spin doctors aim to control the media's access to their clients, and that makes even the most open politician have to struggle to get a clear connection to their public. Some of the older politicians I've worked with are very good at Second Circle connection, but they come from a period when they spoke live at huge rallies and were heckled. Heckling is great training for Second Circle; in fact, this active Second Circle challenge is probably essential for anyone seeking power. Nowadays politicians speak words written for them, which requires tremendous skill to render from Third into Second; if they are not speaking from their hearts, they can only summon passion in Third.

The image makers go to work on politicians and restrict them, demanding a cosmetic presentation rather than an in-the-moment Second Circle one. "Stand like this, don't move your hands, wear this, smile, don't show your teeth, use a more friendly accent," and so on. A good example of this is Al Gore, who came across badly when he campaigned in the 2000 presidential elections as he wasn't allowed to come into his Second Circle with the American public.

So, here is the problem for the politician. How do you stay in Second when you are told to speak generally, not specifically, about things; to control your views and passion; and to toe the party line?

Many politicians go into politics with a passion and desire to make the world better. They start in Second with ideals and passions. They move and excite the electorate with their Second Circle presence, and then lose it as they gradually lose those ideals.

Some politicians enter politics with less shining motives. They are the power-hungry ones in a constituency or state that votes them in regardless of their presence. This breed of politician need never be in Second Circle, as only a Third Circle energy is required to propel them into power.

You rarely meet a First Circle politician, unless they are tired and close to the end of their career.

Impassioned young politicians start their careers in pursuit of the truth. The loss of that passion begins when they meet a variety of obstacles. Often in order to further their career they have to compromise their beliefs. The passion that helped them work in Second and made them noticed by their party and electorate in the first place fades, if not dies.

Then there are the pressures of being interviewed on television and radio. The more you can stay in Second on TV or radio the better, but it is a finely tuned speaker that manages to do so. The usual inclination is to fall back into First and not work enough, believing that technology will do the job. A politician has more reason to move into Third when being interviewed than most, as these people are constantly aware that they could be attacked. Third is a great defense, but the speaker appears aggressive and less caring. It is a courageous politician who manages to stay in Second under attack!

The young politician's openness clashes with the old warhorses of the party, most of whom—battle-scarred and bludgeoned by the media—have adopted Third Circle. Most politicians start their office in Second, but over the years you can see them build up the defenses of Third Circle. For example, when Tony Blair began his career in politics, he was in Second Circle: he met people in Second and was voted into office in Second; but as he felt more threatened by the media and his own party, he disappeared behind the wall of Third Circle.

Most political arenas are gladiatorial settings—the House of Commons is a space that encourages full frontal combat, and even when spaces have been designed to be more generous, to a curved or rounded configuration as in both houses of the U.S. Congress, the size makes many feel threatened.

All these obstacles are magnified for women in politics. Women excel at one-to-one Second Circle, but it is much harder for them to work confrontational spaces in Second. As women they feel more threatened and are tempted to imitate all the negative Third Circle masculine qualities.

This understandable scenario is fatal because it is easy for the public to find the hardness and aggression displayed by women in a heightened Third Circle unattractive. The media can exploit this energy and suggest that we don't trust or like a "cold, hard woman." Men heightening Third Circle can survive longer without the accompanying criticism.

I urge politicians to understand that if you adopt Third Circle, you might appear superficially strong, but there is a loss of human connection between you and the people you govern. Of course, you have to defend yourself sometimes in Third, but aim to return to yourself–and us–in Second. I know you rush around, juggling event after event, meeting hundreds of people every week, and Second Circle costs more than the superficial charm of Third; but try to find time to return to Second.

Many techniques are required to survive TV, the press, and your party; but learn to deal with them in Second Circle. I know how skilled you need to be if you want to stay connected in Second Circle–it is so much quicker and easier to slip into Third.

One young minister I coach appeared on an extremely influential news show and asked one of the older–and very famous– members of his party for advice. The advice was simple: This show is important, so take two days off to prepare. That is, don't bluff it out in Third Circle.

I urge the public to demand that our leaders–the people who decide our fate–are engaged and connected in Second Circle. Do not trust anyone who cannot obtain and sustain that energy and can only speak in Third. If they cannot meet us as an equal in Second Circle, we should withdraw our vote because they don't deserve it.

Watch your leaders carefully. Are they mostly in First? This shows overconfidence and a disregard for the public. They are signalling that they don't have to work to keep us interested. In Third Circle they are defensive, arrogant, or at worst uncaring. Are they ever in Second? What places them there? Anger? Shock? Concern? Or humanity? When confronted, where do they go? It is a good sign if they struggle to stay in Second. At least they are trying to be honest.

Healers

There was a time when doctors were trained not only in science but in the humanities. This produced more doctors with what was called a bedside manner. They could effectively communicate and listen to their patients, showing care and compassion to those who were suffering. They acknowledged their patients' despair.

There was a time when doctors and midwives knew their patients and their family histories and had time to speak to them fully. A lot of the cure was in speaking about the problem. The patient knew their healer and felt known. If a doctor knows the patient, it is easier to be patient with them.

Sadly, this situation has all but disappeared. The training of doctors no longer has much space for talk, care, or sympathy. Directives mean that doctors have to allocate minutes for consultations, even though the evidence is clear that if they spent more time with their patients, a higher proportion would not need extra visits. This is particularly true for those with maladies connected to depression.

It is easy for healers to forget the human being in the healing process. No one can effectively and wholly heal without being present with the patient. Of course, as you are rushed into the Emergency Room you just want the doctor and nurses fully present with the process of saving you; but in calmer moments, Second Circle is essential and imperative to all of us. No one wants a superior or disconnected healer, yet many patients get such treatment when they are at their most vulnerable.

So much medicine today is reliant on high-tech procedures that the doctor or nurses treat their patients like machines, in First or Third. This high technology should not be an excuse to treat people in such a desensitized way. No one wants such treatment, especially when ill or in pain. One of the reasons so many people are flocking to alternative medicine is to experience more presence and kind attention from those who work with the whole Second Circle energy of their patients.

I understand why doctors fail to do this—they are rushed, and it is emotionally easier not to get involved. You will often hear young medics blame their appalling pranks and dehumanizing behavior on the pressure of their job. They meet death and pain every day and need to escape these realities by ridiculing themselves and their patients as a form of balance. But this type of behavior can only dehumanize them and their connections further. The relief, in the work, will be in moments of real connection to their patients, rather than in humiliating them and themselves by a disconnecting mockery that is fundamentally inexcusable.

To the healer, I say this. In Second Circle, you will diagnose better; your mind will go beyond the obvious and perhaps save more lives; the patient will trust you; and that trust will aid you and their healing. A sick, distressed human being has a right to real Second Circle contact and comfort from their healer. The person who holds the dignity of the sick in their hands should be positively present.

It made my mother's last journey bearable for her and her family that one of her night nurses treated her with Second Circle dignity. Her touch and voice created a calm and loving atmosphere that I knew my mother felt, and in this way she was really nursed.

> The art of medicine consists in amusing the patient while nature cures the disease.   —VOLTAIRE

Of course, life-threatening and terrible news should be given in Second Circle. A professional healer cannot seem casual (First) or pompous (Third) in such a situation. After all, distressed people need human contact, not just drugs.

The profession must train doctors, nurses, and paramedics to communicate in Second Circle. Actually, paramedics are some of the most skilled Second Circle communicators. They have probably learned this by trial and error. When an ambulance arrives on any scene, there are usually people in need of immediate help who are enormously agitated. The most efficient way, under these circumstances, to calm someone down and save their life is to adopt Second Circle energy throughout the body, breath, and voice. These are the skills you find among paramedics.

It will help healers if they can clean their energy after work so they don't take home all the pain and distress experienced during their shift. This cleansing exercise can be found in the last chapter of the book, "Daily Practice."

Your Role as a Patient

As a patient, you must try and stay in Second Circle with anyone who treats you, and demand that they speak to you directly and clearly in Second. This is hard if you are lying on your back listening to a discussion about you that is taking place without you! But try saying, "Talk to me, please." Hundreds of doctors have never been called to attention in this way.

A friend of mine recently had an eye operation, which meant she had to remain conscious during surgery. She asked one of the nurses to hold her hand. The effect was to place her attention on another person, and center her. She told me later that she thought of those victims of 9/11 who had to jump from the World Trade Center—many did so holding hands with strangers. In this way they remained present and connected to the end.

When doctors use jargon, ask them to explain in Second Circle language. Avoid moving into Third Circle aggression and stay firm but gracious.

Religious Guides

> Religion . . . in the infinite extent of the universe, is a direc-
> tion of the heart.   —RAINER MARIA RILKE, *Selected Letters*

There was a time when every individual had a Second Circle
connection to their religious elder—their priest, monk, or rabbi.
In this way, baptisms, marriages, and funerals were very personal events.

For many of us, this is no longer the case as we may even
attend important sacred rituals that are being performed by an
individual who doesn't know the person they are baptizing,
marrying, or burying. It is now a rare priest who can perform a
service in Second Circle; hence the many funeral stories of the
priest getting the name or even the sex of the deceased wrong.

The job description of any religious guide involves being able
to address large groups of people and also give comfort to individuals. Both activities would transform the message and the
listener if the wisdom was delivered in Second Circle.

At the heart of all holy scriptures is a necessity for the physical precision of the Word, which, after all, embodies sacred
truth, love, and empathy. These are all Second Circle qualities;
any text and its delivery becomes redundant if deenergized in
First or overblown in Third. If religion is seeking the divine, that
can surely only be pursued in Second, and the central message
of love has to be practiced on earth with Second Circle humanity to others.

It is alarming that many religious leaders are rarely seen in
Second Circle. It is as if they cannot come down to the level of
their fellow human beings, but feel above or removed from us.
You should therefore suspect any religious doctrine spouted in
Third Circle or mumbled in First.

Notice the Third Circle rantings of the fundamentalists, who
seem to have no problem in condemning anyone who disagrees

with them to death and hell. Then listen to the gurus who feel so sure of their doctrine that they speak very quietly in First, so that you have to bow down to hear.

Second Circle can be hard with faith, partly because it honors others around you. The honoring doesn't mean you have to agree, but you do have to try to understand and stay, even for a few minutes, with beliefs that make you uncomfortable. That staying is an act of Second Circle humanity and would probably make the Divine smile.

> And my ending in despair,
> Unless I be reliev'd by prayer,
> Which pierces so that it assaults
> Mercy itself, and frees all faults.
> As you from crimes would pardoned be,
> Let your indulgence set me free.
> —William Shakespeare, *The Tempest*

> The quality of Mercy is not strain'd,
> It droppeth as the gentle rain from heaven
> Upon the place beneath. It is twice blest:
> It blesseth him that gives and him that takes.
> —William Shakespeare,
> *The Merchant of Venice*

32

Leisure

We have so little time for leisure or recreational events, it is not surprising that many of them actually cannot occur in Second Circle. The price of daily life, the need to get the most out of every situation, creates tension in our leisure time. So here are a few strategies for those events we should enjoy but often dread.

Parties

Entering the room. Most of us dread arriving at a party, hovering in the doorway waiting for someone to notice us so that we can acknowledge them.

If no one does, you have to make difficult decisions. Do you push your way into an animated group and introduce yourself? Do you track down a drink to lubricate the mounting pressure of humiliation and hope that as you cross the room someone will stop you and invite you in? Do you fasten a Second Circle focus on a convenient picture and pretend it has your full attention?

In this state you become clear prey for the most boring person at the party: if you are not armed, you can spend the rest of the party stuck in their company.

The panic of parties can easily force you into either an over-enthusiastic and clumsy Third Circle or a defeated wallflower in First.

Next time you enter a room, observe the group objectively. Most active partygoers are in Third, not really relating, but holding court to a group of First Circle listeners who are glad to be included, or those who are facing off in Third with the dominant member of the group. Of course, all this is heightened by alcohol and loud music.

Any group or couple in Second together is engaged, and a heightened engagement will be impenetrable to your presence. If, however, a group is in Second with a present ease, this group is the most likely to let you in, and they will be aware if you are near them in Second. However, a couple in Second Circle may not welcome your presence.

When entering a room, stay in Second and breathe the space. It is quite possible that this will get you noticed and immediately accepted into the party.

Do everything in Second—finding a drink, crossing the room, waiting beside a group—and if people don't respond after a few moments, move on. Sit, if need be, but by staying in Second you won't feel stupid on your own as you would being lonely in First or arrogant and aloof in Third. By staying in Second, someone will notice you and your party will start.

If you get stuck with a bore, be direct, stay in Second, then make your excuses and move off with Second Circle focus. This is better and less rude than staying with them, withdrawing to First, or scanning the room in Third. Bores are not generally attracted to clear presence as they want to hold court in Third Circle energy.

Introduce yourself in Second Circle, but it is probably not advisable to kiss strangers in Second Circle, even on the cheek, which is why air-kissing (Third) has arrived: many people are kissing those they don't want to kiss!

If partygoers become too intoxicated or loud, the only way to survive is to go into Third. Many people enjoy parties in Third as it can be a release, although not for the neighbors! Generalized sex, laughter, drinking, shouting, and dancing are a purge; but don't expect an intimate exchange. However, if you should happen to get one, it is like cool water in the desert.

If you can't join a party in Third, avoid staying and going into First, as this will only depress you. Observing a bit from the sidelines in Second can be educational, and you might attract a fellow present being. If not, the party will begin to feel savage, so it's best just to leave.

Dinner parties. In a strange way, the more intimate the party, the more difficult feeling at ease can be. Stay in Second and listen.

It is easy to make clumsy mistakes in Third because you jump into these intimate parties before you have a chance to assess what is going on. Don't be drawn into competing with others in Third, or ignoring those in First. A Third Circle aggressor is more easily dealt with in Second, and you may be able to draw others out of First if you have Second Circle presence.

Stay in Second during the meal. If you don't know how to eat a particular dish or what utensils to use, watch in Second and you will soon learn.

The good host. Good hosts remain in Second throughout the party—they are on duty and must remain present.

The duties of a host include introducing people; noticing who is not involved and drawing them into the party; moving through the party and checking that everyone has what they need. These duties can only be properly carried out in Second.

Good hosts are present at their party but unable to relax into First Circle or brave it out in Third as they will lose sensitivity to their guests' needs.

The old etiquette books would describe a great host as "gracious." Grace is a Second Circle quality because care about others can only happen when you are present to other people's needs.

Offensive jokes. I'm sure that at some time you have heard an offensive joke. Either the joke hurts you directly or you are aware that it is hurting someone in the group. If you are aware of that direct or indirect hurt, you are in Second Circle. The choice then is either to move away into First or Third to minimize the pain, or stay in Second Circle and perhaps challenge the perpetrator.

If you are telling a joke that offends and you are unaware of its painful consequences until informed later by others, you are probably in Third or First Circle. If you are in Second Circle, then you are knowingly being offensive.

Wedding Speeches

You know the scene—if you haven't been through it, you have watched it enacted in movies: the best man's speech.

He is normally scared and also has had too much to drink to try to calm his nerves. Both tend to place us in Third Circle, so he is blissfully unaware of the reactions of the guests. He starts to tell embarrassing and crude stories about his best friend, the groom. Few of the guests laugh, but he stumbles on. The guests shuffle and fidget themselves out of Second Circle, and as the stories grow dirtier, people leave or start other conversations to push him away. If anyone in the assembly stays present, they might call out and silence him.

If the best man is present, he would change his material at the first sense of unease or lack of laughter. What could be spoken and received in Second Circle at the stag night doesn't translate to the wedding party. And his lack of attention could possibly ruin the wedding, if not the marriage!

Good Service

You are bound to get better service if you negotiate in Second Circle with those who are serving you.

If you have spent any time being a waiter, receptionist, salesperson, or taxi driver yourself, you will know how lonely the job is when those you serve either ignore you in First—actually talking as though you weren't there—or perhaps or worse, patronize and talk down to you in Third.

Of course, as a member of the service industry, you should be attentive in Second all the time. This gets harder when you feel so palpably dehumanized, and can encourage acts of bad service or utter sabotage.

Years ago, a tea lady in a theatre management office admitted to me that I was the only one in the building whose tea she hadn't flicked cigarette ash into. Apparently, because I knew her name, I was saved from her spite!

I remember at drama school, when young students were auditioned, the staff would ask the secretary who processed them as they entered the building, "How did so-and-so behave to you?" The badly behaved or rude students weren't offered a place. I ask my secretary the same question, particularly if I'm not sure whether I want to work with someone.

Remember, everyone wants to be appreciated, whatever their job. If someone does a good job for you, recognize the service in Second Circle.

As a customer, you can reward good service by being in Second with the other person. Instead of shouting at the bad server in Third, try this: go against your instincts by aiming to humanize the grumpy waiter, the casual receptionist, or the aloof salesperson with a direct Second Circle dialogue. There is no need to flatter or be nice; just ask their name and make eye contact (but don't flirt). Assume they can be better at their job. Mean "please" and "thank you" if you are in Second Circle, and if they do anything right, praise them. If they continue to be rude, then you have a right to complain.

You will get far better service if you approach people in Second; and if you have regular contact with them, you will create an ally, not an enemy.

33

Cleansing Your Negative Energy

This chapter provides a very simple but extremely profound exercise to return your body and breath to a clean place after distress.

I suggest that you use this exercise to help regulate and clear your body and breath of the physical manifestations of pain and the locks that such pain creates.

The exercise is also useful if you have to deal with the pain and distress of others.

We all take on the physical habits of those around us and other people's emotional distortions can embed themselves in our bodies.

Some professionals are very prone to this exchange, which is why they might choose not to exist in Second Circle. Obvious examples are health workers who, on a daily level, deal with the death and pain of others. Law enforcers have death, rage, and despair thrown at them hourly. Teachers struggle in violent schools with the constant threat of aggression. Anyone who deals with the aggravation of customers or colleagues will also have that energy embedded in them.

My advice to these professionals is to take time to do this exercise at least once a week, to clean this negative energy out of you and avoid bringing it home into the rest of your life. Not only will you feel better, but you will be able to deal more freely in Second Circle within your job. This will make you much better at your job without its destroying and debilitating you.

The Exercise

This will take about twenty minutes. Feel free to cry, wail, or get angry as the release works. You should also feel free to stop the exercise if it becomes too hard to bear.

- Find a safe and private place.
- Adopt the deep release position. Lie on your back with a small cushion under your head. Your calf muscles should rest comfortably supported by a chair, with your thighs at right angles to the floor. Unclamp your thighs and release your shoulders. Place one hand just above your groin as this will help to locate the breath.

The aim of the exercise is to calm the breath down to its deepest and slowest position, without any locks or holds. The breath will then be able to cleanse your body and disperse negative energy lodged within you.

- Start the exercise by imagining a calm and beautiful natural setting. Place your mind onto that setting. Use music if it helps.
- Now, gently and freely and without much sound, sigh out. Continue the sigh without strain until you feel nothing left in you. This is the only sigh you use in the exercise.
- When the breath has been expired, wait until the body wants to breathe in. Think of this waiting as a fluid suspension, not a hold.
- As you start to breathe in, do so silently and slowly.
- At the point you feel full, don't lock the breath but suspend it until the body wants to breathe out.

- As you breathe out, go to the end of the breath and sus-pend it until you again slowly and silently breathe in.
- Continue this breath pattern for as long as you can (20 minutes is ideal).
- Concentrate on the breath. Empty your mind and heart.
- Get up slowly and either go straight to bed or come back to the world gradually. You will be in First Circle, but come up slowly and focus on specific points in the room. This will draw you into a very gentle Second Circle without any of the day's distortion.

34
Daily
Practice

The readiness is all.
—WILLIAM SHAKESPEARE, *Hamlet*

The last word of Colette, the brilliant French novelist, was "Look." In your daily practice, connect to detail. Look, listen, think, and feel detail.

Really connect with the bird's eye, the leaf's formation, the petals of a flower, the stain on the carpet or the wall, the crack in the pavement, a cloud formation, the shadow on the wall. Look at a loved one and see their eyes—the fear, the love in them—the hair on their collar; their hand. Hear the sound of their breath; their voice. Hear the music.

Think about an idea, its newness, its shock, or the heart, and what exactly you are feeling.

Living in an urban setting in the twenty-first century reduces your chance of being present. There is too much noise, rush, information—and so many people. We have too little space or time for nature and silence. You must perform a daily practice or ritual to stay connected. Here are some suggestions.

Physical Practices

- Center your body every morning before you face the world. Your shoulders, upper chest, and jaw should be released. Hold your spine up and release the abdominal muscles.

Keep your knees unlocked and your feet firmly on the
ground—feel the floor through the balls of your feet.

- Walk with direct energy. Try to walk in nature every few
days.
- Stretch the sides and back of your rib cage. Breathe low
and silently to a focus outside your window.
- Warm up your voice with gentle humming or singing.

Senses

- Taste food in Second.
- Identify a new smell in your world.
- Look at nature—a flower, a tree, a bird.
- Notice the weather.
- Look up at the moon and stars.
- Listen to one item on the news with your full attention.
- Listen to a new style of music.
- Shower or bathe in Second.

Mind

- Read an article in a newspaper that you don't normally read.
- Read a poem out loud and don't be frightened if you don't
fully understand it.
- Ask yourself and others around you for an opinion about
the top story in the news.

Heart

- Ask yourself what you are feeling.
- Acknowledge different feelings you experience during the
day, be they fear, joy, or panic.
- On a typical day you can connect to the world and make
your day more meaningful by: noticing babies and animals; talking to your child without the aid of toys and
TV—even for a few minutes make them the center of your
world; socializing in quiet surroundings.

On waking

- Notice the room, the day, the weather, the bed, the person beside you, in Second Circle.
- Try not to turn on the TV or radio unless you spend some time listening in Second to a music or news item.
- Talk to your partner and children in Second before you move into your day.
- Taste your morning drink and breakfast in Second Circle.
- Breathe in Second before you leave your home.

On journeys

- Notice the world outside yourself.
- Change routes to keep interested.
- Look up as you walk and notice the world above you. Look at the sky in Second Circle.
- Don't always travel wired up to an iPod.
- In the car, drive sometimes without the radio and, when you stop, reconnect to the world by checking it out in Second Circle.
- Be gracious to other drivers: let them out of side turnings when appropriate, and try to catch human contact with them. Do the same for pedestrians.
- Thank others if they do the same for you.
- Walk upstairs and push doors open in Second Circle.
- Try not to use your cell phone too frequently.

At work

- Make Second Circle contact with the first person you can as you enter the building and receive any contact back.
- Read reports, make telephone conversations, write e-mails and texts in Second Circle.
- Conduct any important meeting or interview in Second Circle.
- Listen in Second before you give an opinion.

- Even in a noisy work environment, try to stay in Second for any important exchanges.

At the end of the day, reconnect to your breath and body. Relax and clean your energy if it has been a difficult day (see page 253).

New Beginnings

Cherish the moments when you feel the surge of Second Circle energy and, as you finish this book, stay present. You are now starting a journey back to the beginning of your presence that can take you to the end. Remember, you are much more alive and brilliant than you have allowed yourself to be.

About the Author

Patsy Rodenburg, OBE, is recognized as one of the world's leading voice and acting coaches. She is the founder of the Voice Department at London's Royal National Theatre and runs the Voice Department at the Guildhall School of Music and Drama. She was the voice coach at the Royal Shakespeare Company in London for nine years and has taught voice and presence for all the leading theatre companies in the world. Her film credits include collaborations with such directors as Mike Nichols, Franco Zeffirelli, and Sam Mendes. Patsy's work has extended beyond the theatre, including teaching voice and communication to business executives and lecturing on vocal care and listening skills at the Royal College of Surgeons in London. She has given courses for teachers and politicians and has taught Shakespeare as Therapy in British prisons.

Visit her Web site at www.patsyrodenburg.com.